Praise for

HONEY IS THE KNIFE

Hannah Eko's sparkling debut, *Honey Is the Knife*, is part homage, part resistance, part love letter, and part road map from bounded to unbounded Black woman thinking. At its core is Òsun, the Yoruba goddess, and how the goddess can inspire daughters of the diaspora. Eko has assembled a multifaceted anti-self-help manifesto that reconsiders and reconfigures a popular and problematic genre. It's an earnest and vulnerable work written in service of what Angela Davis has called "freedom practice." Influential luminaries like bell hooks, Ntozake Shange, and Sojourner Truth (to name a few) inform Eko's book, which honors her ancestors and holds its own, leading the way for a new generation. Do not let this sweetness pass you by!

—Yona Harvey, poet, Kate Tufts Discovery award winner, and author of *Hemming the Water* and *You Don't Have to Go to Mars for Love*

Honey Is the Knife is an intricately fashioned, profoundly moving book. In this work, Hannah Eko presents a collection of nonfiction that you'll want to sit with for days, savoring the nuance and wonder of every word. The language is toothy and raw, and it is a special thing to find a writer so gifted and committed to expressing the self. Eko does this skillfully, carefully, with exacting precision. *Honey Is the Knife* is astounding, and Hannah Eko is a phenomenal writer.

—Kristen Arnett, *New York Times* best selling writer and author of *Mostly Dead Things* and *With Teeth: A Novel*

Honey Is the Knife is a necessary and transparent collection of essays that explores the relationship between pleasure and pain, strength and sorrow, grief and healing (and more). From Oprah to Òsun, Eko seamlessly weaves the personal with popular culture. Her writing serves as a mirror that invites readers to reflect on their own experiences with honesty and vulnerability.

—Charlesia McKinney, PhD and Scholar of Pleasure Literacies, Pedagogies of Pleasure, Black Feminist Pleasure Politics

Honey Is the Knife is an anthem for Black women. Eko incisively and generously shares her journey and wisdom on loving one's self and sharing just how she has arrived to centering pleasure, self-care, and truth telling. A well-researched feast, full of insights about colorism, feminism, alternative modes of healing, and spirituality, this book is the perfect gift for sisters, friends, lovers, and aunties who need a salve in these trying moments. Honest and illuminating!

—Angie Cruz, author of *Soledad*, *Let It Rain Coffee*, and the YA/ALSA winning novel *Dominicana*

Spiritual, carnal, erudite, and exquisitely original, *Honey Is the Knife* is a balm and a treasure, a luminous book to be savored. Hannah Eko's deep love for Black women imbues every line. She wants the best for us, wants us to be pleasure-centered. And for those of us who need a map to get there, Eko is that gentle, vulnerable guide walking alongside us in these pages. I am smarter, more compassionate with myself, and more in awe of myself, for having read this beautiful book.

—Deesha Philyaw, National Book Award Finalist and PEN Faulkner Award winning author of *The Secret Lives of Church Ladies*

HONEY IS THE KNIFE

HONEY IS THE KNIFE

OR HOW I LEARNED TO STOP FIXING MYSELF AND LOVE MY BLISS

BY

HANNAH EKO

Library of Congress Control Number: 2024903066
ISBN Hardcover: 979-8-9904097-0-5

First Edition 2024

To Dayo, Bukky, and all the lost daughters...
May you rest in peace, power, and pleasure.

"She found a taste for cold things that released their sweetness slowly—ice cream that slid down her throat before she could taste it, tinned peaches in chill syrup.

"But there was no heart there in her chest."

—Helen Oyeyemi, *Mr. Fox*

"She was stretched on her back beneath the pear tree soaking in the alto chant of the visiting bees, the gold of the sun and the panting breath of the breeze when the inaudible voice of it all came to her. She saw a dust-bearing bee sink into the sanctum of a bloom; the thousand sister-calyxes arch to meet the love embrace and the ecstatic shiver of the tree from root to tiniest branch creaming in every blossom and frothing with delight. So this was a marriage! She had been summoned to behold a revelation. Then Janie felt a pain remorseless sweet that left her limp and languid."

—Zora Neale Hurston, *Their Eyes Were Watching God*

CONTENTS

Introduction

You were made to follow your bliss—to melt into the sweet honey of your peace, power, and pleasure with zero apology. You were made to alchemize your shame, suffering, and struggle into bliss. Maybe something in you protests this notion, thinking I am being naïve, a tad too New Age guru. So, let me say it again for your inner Sad Girl: you deserve to feel good, to heal deeply, to exist as exactly who you are. You do not have to do anything to earn bliss or wait until you or this world has reached peak perfection to feel it. And yes, I know the world is currently embroiled in a poly-crisis of epic proportions. I know how deeply racism, sexism, queerphobia, inter-generational trauma, hatreds, wars, and violences spanning the petty and the brutal endure. I know how much people like you and me are expected to give and how little we are expected to receive in return. I know that your life has obligations and limitations and heavy histories. I know that it is not easy to change.

Bliss is not "indefinitely improve your productivity" or "become a re-spectable saint." Bliss isn't even about reading more feminist theory or marching down city avenues. Following your bliss is about gifting yourself the same sweetness that you so easily offer to everyone else, being brave enough to go deep within, falling in love with the complexity of your humanity beyond the roles assigned you. Following your bliss is never forgetting that your honey, your peace, power, and pleasure, is your best defense in a world gone mad.

I don't think it was an accident that I fell in love with the sweetness of Òsun knee-deep into the summer of 2016, one year after leaving my active duty Coast Guard life and two semesters into my grad school degree. I am an eldest Nigerian-American daughter, trained by interests both foreign and domestic to put others before me. If there were ever a candidate for someone who needed an influx of honey, it was me. I met the soul of Òsun four months before Trump took office and regressed the world into the recesses of his underdeveloped psyche, four years before COVID-19 drowned our lives in mask mandates, social distancing, and sourdough.

Òsun is the grand seductress of life itself, a goddess who beckons us to dance to a new yet ancient song. Hailing from the Yoruba tribe of southwest Nigeria, she has made her way around the world and across many waters. Òsun is a generous West African feminine deity who rules over fertility, sweet waters, divination, creativity, and love. She teaches me time and time again that life is here to be enjoyed.

I was thirty years old, nervously alive, and eager to visit Nigeria, the land that makes me possible—a land that I, as part of the "lost generation" (African kids raised outside the continent), had never visited before and only knew from my parents' stories. For six magically messy weeks, I studied the feminine deities of the Yoruba tradition, attended the centuries-old festival, and drank more Origin beer than is probably ladylike.

When my finger skated across the words "honey is the knife" in a soft yellow research book, I dog-eared the top-left corner and chewed on those five delicious syllables for months. "Honey is the knife" is an extension of Lucumi praise literature, Lucumi being one of the many Yoruba-derived spiritualities still alive today. Charles Abramson, a gifted African American artist, demonstrated his love for Òsun with a gorgeous altar in his Brooklyn studio. In one of his final conversations before passing into the next world, he shared, "With Òsun you know that honey is the knife." She does not defend herself with assault rifles or with swords but with her honey, her sweetness.

I have a vexed relationship with sweetness and bliss, desirous and suspicious of feeling good in equal measure, like I am forever pressing both accelerator and brake simultaneously. I did not trust life to be kind unless I was perfection in Black girl form. My addiction to the promises of flawlessness began in third grade when I bought *How to Whistle* for ninety-nine cents from the Scholastic Book Fair. I wanted to whistle like one of those skipping children of daytime TV, so I bought a book that promised to teach me how.

I never quite mastered whistling (to this day I sort of sound like a broken tea kettle), but I count this emaciated book as the beginning of my lifelong quest to correct whatever personal defect I could find. I believed there was something wrong with me—some indelible inner mistake that only outer perfection could alleviate. Fixing myself—and by extension, the world—became an obsessive zeal and ate up a lot of time. I chaired diversity boards, wrote a thesis on racial equity, tried (and failed) to start a Black Hair revolution in the Coast Guard. I went on shamanic journeys in sweaty yoga studios, walked on a mini-pilgrimage to the Black Madonna of Montserrat, spent ten *vipassana* meditation days in the Washington wilderness, forced myself to love the taste of uncooked kale. Numerology, Bible study, Human Design, Myers-Briggs, Strengths Finder—if there's a promise of self-actualization in there, I have probably done it.

I have been in therapy long enough to contextualize why I tumbled headfirst into the Church of Eternal Self-Improvement: my stubborn Aries sun, social/familial/political trauma, first generation displacement, and a highly sensitive nervous system with a gift of imagining catastrophe. In my late teens, I nicknamed the freezing anxiety I felt inside the Block. Self-help was a haven that promised resolution and deliverance into a cloud of safety from this Block. Follow this top-knot hippie with the 500k followers and beatific smile. Change your mindset in three-easy steps for $797 per month. Take this 88-question quiz and you will discover your Feminine Archetype and free yourself from this existential, traumatic experience called life.

I am a daughter of the 1990s, the era of Positive Self-Esteem, participation trophies, and Oprah Winfrey gifting Pontiacs on primetime TV. I suckled at the breast of *The Book of Virtues*. Growing up in Southern California, the epicenter of the New Age guru, I experienced my coming of age as juxtaposed with self-help classics like *Codependent No More* and

Fat Is a Feminist Issue. I was a good kid desiring to be perfect, a third grader who poured over Proverbs and Psalms until their gold-rimmed pages curled like spirals.

My fascination with self-improvement was also baked into being by an American culture eager to medicate trauma and fear with three-act redemptive arcs and rags-to-riches tales. Who needs more promise of golden tomorrows than a super nation of outcasts, pilgrims, kidnappees, explorers, runaways, and refugees trying to outrun their internal turmoil and PTSD? The genre of self-help is an extension of Christianized notions of perfected purity made famous by Dale Carnegie of *How to Win Friends and Influence People* fame and mystics like Florence Scovel Schinn, who wrote *The Game of Life.*

As much as I bristled at these titles and their almost pathological ignorance of systemic oppression, I cannot even front: I wanted the heaven they were promising. I hoped that one day, kinda like some Blackgirl Moses, I would emerge from Wellness Mountaintop, without intestinal distress, generalized anxieties, or feminist rage with a gravity defying ass and the ability to speak fluent Spanish and Yoruba. Suffice to say—this day has not arrived. This is not the kind of book where I promise make-over magic because I know how you feel about the words *self-help.* The majority of our current "wellness" culture is authored by the politically ignorant who casually equate darkness with evil and name their deep-set denial "staying positive." This brand of personal transformation is predatory, fantasy based and pathological, preying on the most vulnerable and ignoring significant historical, emotional, and spiritual trauma.

I believe in the power of transformation. I also believe that circumstances, often beyond our control, highly influence what we can do, have, and achieve, sometimes monstrously so. I don't believe we can really achieve what we desire without sweetness, without honey and our bliss as our lubricant. I do *not* believe we arrive on this planet full of mistakes or that I must pay rent for taking up space in this world. I do not believe our progress towards sweetness is always linear. I do not believe our humanity is an ugly machine requiring fixing. I do not believe a Black woman is destined to clean up the world's mess.

Fixing implies there is something wrong with us and deepens the idea that our present tense existence is an existential mistake. Fixing places the blame on the shoulders of the survivor while abusers are allowed lifetimes to fuck up. Many of us have been socialized and rewarded for tending and befriending everyone but ourselves, a scam of ancestral proportions. We do not need any more wounded healers attempting to save the world while negating themselves. We are chock full, abundant in self-sacrifice and self-loathing. We need a buzz of women who dare to remember that life is sweet and bravely follow their bliss however and wherever they can.

You were born to make manifest the beauty inside of you, and we don't do this by chasing perfection or arguing against reality. Clearly, this world is not a perfect place that forever makes sense. You co-create with what is—the mess and the beauty, the honey and the knife, for all that we are will always lead to love.

You are here to remember that your original form is bliss and that you are bliss still.

And that bliss is just another name for love.

All emotions lead to love, be they rage or ecstasy, despair or calm.

Everything—from a bad mood to a lick of the Atlantic ocean—is just love in another form. *Honey Is the Knife* rests upon *alchemy*, a transmutation, a melting of shame, suffering, and struggle into peace, power, and pleasure. There is no end state, just a vast continuum, a connecting to the stories that our blood holds close. Our sweet actualization is the Sagrada Família, an awe-inspiring cathedral that we may not live to see completed.

We show up for our sweetness and our bliss anyways.

Most self-help books start with some panic-inducing premise about there being Something Deeply Wrong™ with you that only their One True Method™ can repair. Each author was once an addicted, self-hating lump of human tissue until they hit Rock Bottom™ and went on a Life-

Changing Journey™ and now they're vegan millionaires and it's their *duty* to share their One True Message™ and Save The World©.

I do not have that story. First off, Black women have enough work. Adding "save the world" to my to-do list is not my idea of a good time.

My life is rich and real. I am deeply honored to be here on this planet even on my worst days. I have beautiful relationships with my friends and family, I do work I love, and every year I get better at loving who I am and doing what I can, from where I am, with what I have. And sometimes, I too desire to rocket myself to the Octavia Butler Landing Space on the planet Mars and never return to earth again.

If you picked up this book eager to "fix" yourself or save the world, knife in hand, I have very bad news for you: this book is not it. I have *zero* idea what perfection looks like in the Anthropocene and I do not pretend to know what the future holds or have some Messiah complex. But, I would rather spend the time I have left on this planet becoming more like bliss and recovering my sweetness one small dose at a time.

Your blocks—the most sensitive areas of your soul—are not an enemy faction. Your specific blocks, which may overlap or be completely divergent of mine, are your unique path to peace, power, and pleasure. Your blocks are hard honey, reactions, and coping mechanisms that are doing their best to protect you from harm. No matter how old these wounds are, no matter who you inherited them from, your sweetness and your bliss is near. After all, honey found thousands of years later has still been found to be edible, still delivering on its sweetness even when one might have expected dust.

If you want your honey to flow, you place it in sweet, warm water.

You let those blocks sit as long as they need.

You make a romance of the waiting.

Your self-recovery path might look a lot like mine did, attacking your flaws like some never-ending renovation project and trying to save the world—though I sincerely hope your self-help journey did not involve as much bad kale or misanthropic activists. Maybe you've read *One Day My Soul Just Opened Up, The Four Agreements, The Body Keeps the Score.* Maybe

8

you sat in a lot of women's circles in your formative years. Maybe you've gone to a lot of therapy. Maybe you're tired and desiring something deeper than performative gestures and half-baked truths.

Honey Is the Knife is harm reduction for the soul,[1] a softcore feminist approach of self-kindness. No harsh penetration, no 180-degree overnight transformations that fall flaccid after a week. *Honey Is the Knife* takes the edible approach: start low, go slow, and watch the magic happen as you become intimate with your entire life. Softly release the idea that you need to save the world, that you are somehow above the hurt that chokes the earth. The only thing you own in this lifetime is you.

Honey Is the Knife is a compassionate pleasure ethic rooted in divine feminine cosmologies,[2] Black feminism, and the radical acceptance that

---

1 "Harm reduction" is a philosophy and public health model often deployed within substance misuse prevention programs to curb overdose deaths, negative social/mental/emotional consequences of substance misuse, and the damage caused by the War on Drugs, especially in Black and Brown communities. Harm reduction is not without its (very loud) critics, but the compassionate realism at the heart of harm reduction (needle exchanges, naloxone, treatment centers, cannabis medicine, psychedelic therapies, etc.) has saved lives due to its focus on valuing the autonomy and safety of people who use drugs. There has been a lot of harm done in the name of self-help and spirituality, from cultish charlatans to abusive missionaries. *Honey Is the Knife* is just one antidote to this legacy.

2 If reading the word Goddess or Divine Feminine makes you want to roll your eyes into 3000 BC and call up Judith Butler, I understand. The Goddess is a difficult concept to grasp, let alone believe in, within the context of patriarchy and overly strict gender binaries. The feminine has been so fucked with, so reduced, that I wonder how much of her energy is performance and how much of her is real sometimes myself. Goddess is simply a two-syllable word used to denote the feminine face of God or a female deity. Divine Feminine is a rebalance of the feminine principle that has been misunderstood and subjected to violence for a really, really long time. The feminine is a continuum, so it might be better to call her Divine Femininities. Feminine describes energy, both material and abstract, which is intuitive, creative, fluid, receptive, dark, cool, and attuned to the deepest self. Think moon, yin, womb, winter, introspection, being-ness, and fall. When the world was but formless dark water (Genesis 1:2), the divine feminine was, is, will be. The three starring Divine Femininities of the Yoruba tradition—Ọya, Òsun, and Yemọja— recast femininity's most maligned traits as tools of self-actualization: anger is passion, nurturing is power, sexuality is liberation. Ọya is a warrior, shape shifter, and goddess of thunder, while Yemọja is mother of fish, guardian of water spirits, raging ocean. Òsun, the most direct inspiration for the pleasure ethic of *Honey Is the Knife*, is the grounded seductress of life itself, vulture woman, healing waters, honey as revolution. Yemọja, Oya, and Òsun are an ancient (contd.)

is kindness. Self-kindness does not mean condoning, liking, or loving everything about yourself or your world 24/7 with a Pollyanna smile and *love and light* affirmations. Kindness simply means acknowledging your *entire* experience and practicing bold, yet accessible movement *towards* your peace, power, and pleasure.

My approach is not for everyone, which I am very cool with. Here's a list of qualities that will make *Honey Is the Knife* the alternative self-help guide for you:

- **You are open-minded.** You love to read and learn and have been described as curious, introverted, spiritual, introspective, or nerdy. You are a modern mystic who loves expanding your consciousness. You do not believe receiving inspiration from Indigenous African cosmology is equivalent to burning in hell.

- **You are a self-love romantic.** You were raised to believe your only role was to serve others: as mother, eager beaver partner, martyr-social-justice-activist-savior. You no longer believe the hype. You are ready to focus on you. You are ready for play and pleasure to be your guide.

- **You are socially aware.** You detest misuses of power like racism, sexism, and the like. You adore nuance. You are eager to create new generational patterns. You believe that the personal is the political and that individual and collective healing go on brunch dates.

- **You are a divine-feminine feminist.** You appreciate the basic tenets of intersectional feminism and love women, the feminine, womanism, the femme. You honor femininities that are not you and those that are non-binary, trans, fluid, and unlabeled. You

---

version of the supergroup TLC, a Crazy/Sexy/Cool of the Divine Feminine set. Heart. Mind. Body. They are a Mother/Lover/Warrior triune of feminine energy reminding us humanoids that feminine power holds a variety of expressions. The Goddess is for everybody and every body. If the word Goddess trips you up, no worries. Think of Her as a verb, the loving expression of your peace, power, and pleasure.

believe a hearty part of your own and the world's development requires healing the ruptures caused by sexism, misogyny, and gendered violence. This is Girl Power for Grown-Ups.

- **You are unconventional.** You hail from the island of misfit Black girls. *Honey Is the Knife* is for the nerds, the queer and queerish, indigo children and electric ladies, the sensitive, weirdos, free-spirits, misfits, and anyone who has ever been called an Oreo.

- **You crave real change.** You bought the Road Opener candles, meditated, attended the wellness pep rallies, and contemplated selling your Honda Accord and moving to an ashram in Thailand. You want to create room for change from exactly where you are.

Òsun is the connective tissue, the undeniable pulse of *Honey Is the Knife*. Whenever I want to indulge in a esoteric pity party, she reminds me that bliss is an option. She reminds me that life is to be enjoyed and celebrated. Òsun helps me dance with my pain and use my honey as a knife. Her most famous stories (these are called *patakís* in the Ifa and Santeria tradition—micro-fables used to impart wisdom) serve as interludes in this book. Òsun is an ancient yet futuristic feminine energy—dark, wild, and sweet. She is an alternative healer who accepts herself just the way she is.

She is a masterful alchemist, changing wounds into honey.

Honey Is the Knife is fifteen eclectic chapters of some of my most personal stories, Black femme nerdiness, and open-ended how-to. My personal stories cover everything from colorism to the mother wound. These are some of my most sensitive spaces that have also coincidentally brought me closer to my sweetness. The sensitive spaces are where the best honey resides.

You do not need to be initiated into an African Traditional Spirituality (Santeria, Candomblé, Ifá, Lucumi, Vodoun, etc.) to receive inspiration from Òsun, but please respect the rituals of those who carry a formalized relationship with Òsun present-tense and of yesteryear.

African spiritual traditions have survived the effects of colonization, racism, ignorance, imperialism, violence, and fear. They are deeply intricate spiritual systems that work with the forces of nature. Their survival alone deserves appreciation, especially since the legacies of these wounds are still very much alive.

You might feel pulled more to some chapters than others. Feel free to read in order or read in roulette style. Geek out on the footnotes, or save them for a rainy day that never arrives. Each section explores the tension between struggle and peace, shame and power, suffering and pleasure. Sit with whatever works for and with your path. Feel free to be choosy.

There are praxis moments throughout the book if you want some pointers on how to *practice* being kinder to yourself. Theory alone can only do so much. You may have wanted to *live* the sweet life for a long time but become overwhelmed by the *how*. The praxis moments are micro-transformations that allow you to practice peace, power, and pleasure in doable ways.

A drop is an accessible practice for the moment.

A drizzle might require an hour or more.

A pour is a heavier investment—weeks, months, years, your entire life.

These praxis moments are *completely* voluntary, but they are there for you should you desire. Your honey is you and you are always enough—whether your honey is hard and crystallizing into sugar, runny like thin string, or a luscious slow pour that feels almost X-rated.

Allow Òsun's paradoxical charm to inspire you, as she continues to inspire me, to bring more bliss, more sweetness to your life. May this book bring you closer to your bliss, to your peace, power, and pleasure just as you are. And may you always know that your honey is the knife.

Peace,

Hannah

P.S. I am a writer. Even though I discuss issues of emotional/spiritual health within this book, no advice or insight within *Honey Is the Knife* should take the place of receiving professional mental health diagnoses, medical interventions, therapy, or counseling. Savor what you like and leave the rest.

Guidance for the Praxis Sections

Honey Is the Knife is a personal, trauma-aware, pleasure-based ethic of self-love, self-recovery, and self-kindness as freedom. An ethic, or practice, aligns your inner values and intentions with outward actions, otherwise known as praxis.

The praxis in this book are simple enough to remember, malleable enough to fine-tune for your unique needs, and fun enough that you don't shout *fuck this, I'm out* after day one.

Praxis is about practicing accessible movements that softly expand your peace, power, or pleasure, moving from shame to power, from struggle to peace, and from suffering to pleasure. This is a practice where your bliss is medicine. It's less 180-degree light-switch flip and more of slow and steady movement in the *direction* of your freedom.

Shame, suffering, and struggle are normal facets of life. It's okay to not be fine all the time. Be patient with your progress and know that each day offers a chance to be good to yourself just as you are.

Keep going. We want all of you here.

To get started, I suggest slowing down enough to be honest about your present-tense experience. You can use the three explorations below as starting points.

- How can you bring more chill to your experience? What helps you feel a sense of **peace**, ease, or calm?
- How can you bring more kindness to your experience? What helps you lean into your **power**, compassion, comfort, and affection?
- How can you bring more sexiness to your experience? What is your **pleasure**? What delights you and makes you come alive?

When you **identify the struggle** between want and need, you move closer to peace. When you **witness your shame without additional shaming**, you move into your personal power. And **reducing your suffering** will make pleasure safe enough for your body, mind, and soul to digest and fully receive—no forced entry required.

Interlude 1

Interlude I:
From Shame to Power

So one day, people were really trying to get Ogun, the orisa of iron, to return to civilization. But Ogun wasn't feeling it. He was going through "some identity stuff" and wasn't sure if he wanted to continue his terms of employment, despite the generous 401(k). The orisas[3] tried all their persuasions (invites to the best feasts, courtside tickets for the fertility festival, yams, etc.). They even tried having some of the other gods go and talk to Ogun, but nothing worked.

Finally, the gods wised up and asked Òsun to go and talk to Ogun. Perhaps as his on-off-again "friend with benefits," she could persuade him? Òsun yawned. So like these gods to only invite her when they needed something. But, she always did like a challenge. She returned home, covered her body with wildflower honey and royal jelly, and paused right by the river (which was also conveniently near Ogun's studio). Sure enough when Ogun saw Òsun in all her glory, he forgot his own name—he was awake.

One of Òsun's mightiest powers is her sexual and sensual energy.

---

3 Orisa is a personification of energy made divine. This energy is referred to in Yoruba as *ase*, which has no direct translation in English and is often closely defined as "and so it is." Existence is an action of holy proportions. Orisa are divine messengers of Olódùmarè, commonly approached as gods and goddesses. They have been transported across the world (mainly due to the transatlantic slave trade and diaspora migrations) where they sometimes have different names. (For instance, Òsun becomes Oshun or Oxum depending if you are referencing the Yoruba, Cuban Santeria, or Brazilian Candomble.) The orisa are thought to be innumerable or to number "400 plus 1" depending on who you hear tell it. They are the sacred intermediaries of Yoruba cosmologies.

Humans, to our deep detriment, have misunderstood, underestimated, and pigeonholed Òsun and her sensual power since she arrived on the scene. Far from being simplistic hyper-promiscuity, sexual energy lies along the same plane as creation, power, and money. Sex is power, and this is why women and gender-expansive beings have been shamed for our sexuality for eons. The world has not been made ready for this power.

But goody for us: where there is shame, there is power. Power is: confidence, security, stability, and the ability to do, be, or have what you (really) want. Great shame and great power are always in relationship, like the bend of umbilical cord.

Òsun never wastes time forcing anyone to her will or convincing anyone that she is powerful. In this story, she embodied who she was. She existed. She covered herself with honey and stood by a tree, her power less domination and more invitation. Òsun teaches us to undertake the vulnerable work of transforming our deepest shames into our deepest powers by choosing to name ourselves in a different way again and again and again.

1

Mirror, Mirror, Down the Hall

In my uncle's house, there was a mirror floating above a jungle of brown carpet. This mirror was tall and slender and outlined with 1980s art deco squiggles in black-and-white. Running down the length of this mirror was a crack, artery thick and bottomless.

I lived with my uncle, aunt, and cousins for several months when I was about six or so years old in between a brief stay in foster care. It was a lonely, confusing time, and I lived for small pleasures. I loved watching myself in that mirror, meeting my growing reflection from one end of the hall to the other.

One day, curious about the line down the middle, I used my finger to trace it. Decades later I can still locate the surprise: the blood, a voluptuous red drip running down my tiny finger single file, the first time a mirror's mysteries demanded payment in flesh.

I was heavily dependent on mirrors to know I was real, but any certainty I felt quickly dissipated as soon as I left the mirror's hold. My gazes into mirrors were often body-critiquing events where I shamed myself for not being Naomi Campbell. But when I was not participating in America's #1 female sport of latent body shame, I really *liked* mirrors. Maybe a bit too much. At ten years old and tasked with babysitting, I'd hold babies up to a mirror, amazed at their inability to recognize themselves. I loved to consider the infinity of myself beyond this rather two-dimensional landscape of cheekbones and full mouth. Who was I beyond the storylines I inherited?

My tendency to check storefront windows, dressing room rectangles, car rearviews, and the eyes of whatever dude I was developing a crush on often felt like a shameful quirk. I felt almost disgust for how much I cared about what others thought of me. I had little idea that positive mirroring was how a person learned to *be*.

We coo and grin with our baby gums; our mothers smile back. We convulse into tears, and our caregivers frown eyebrows in concern. From this almost magical witnessing, we learn that another sees us and knows us and that we are real.

Our mothers and caregivers, powerful but also deeply human, can never be perfect mirrors, only "good enough" ones—their ability to reflect us depends so deeply on their ability to see themselves. If their internal mirror is fogged up by emotional chaos and pain, be mindful: their projections are closer than they appear. The "good enough" mother is a term coined by British psychoanalyst and pediatrician D.W. Winnicott in 1953. The "good enough" mother isn't about excusing abuse or neglect but making space for the reality of imperfect caregiving. In fact, our caregivers *must* fail us in some ways.[4] Their failure reveals our agency, and that is how we learn independence.

We never quite outrun our first mirrors. As we move along, we encounter "other mothers" and find "other mirrors" who add to how we see ourselves and how real we feel. Witness children copying the big kids in their play, and we will see the mirror effect in action. Watch with bemused wonder how we start to dress like our coworkers no matter how much we hate capris. We'll be sitting across a friend at a café and suddenly realize that we are sitting exactly the same, from tilt of chin to lift of elbow.

---

4 bell hooks named this mirror/power structure the "imperialist white supremacist capitalistic patriarchy" within several of her texts. I wonder sometimes just how much to name this collective delusion and when. The imperialist white supremacist capitalistic patriarchy is exhausting as hell and super annoying when it's not being genocidal. Total buzzkill. Sometimes the *thing* needs to be named to be known, and other times naming only further buries the sick ideas of oppression further into our consciousness, becoming the mirror in which we see ourselves and the world. So yeah, sometimes I like to pretend this power structure does not exist.

Moving towards mirror is so subtle that we hardly realize the dance until already in place, hand reaching outward.

When I was in seventh grade, my junior high school group was a good girl consortium of white girls and first-generation Brown daughters tiptoeing to assimilation. I was the dark-skinned Black girl in the group, granted entry because I had a sincere love of Green Day and Freddie Prinze, Jr. These girls—in all their brave and myopic glory—were my mirrors and I was theirs.

Unlike my friends who mostly bought their flared jeans and puka shell necklaces from the Brea Mall, my clothes were a mix of discount stores (all hail TJ Maxx) and the Fashion Alley of Downtown LA. Today, the Alley is haven for hipster artists and in-the-know influencers, but in my adolescent heyday, the Alley was where you shopped if you were broke.

My most frequent purchase in Downtown LA was colored contact lenses. The packages were sold in bulk, probably scalped from some high-end optician's inventory—five packs of green, blue, or violet contacts for $20. The songs I loved praised light eyes as more beautiful and song-worthy than brown ones, making Black girls with hazel or green eyes a genetic treasure. And so, when I could, I'd spend the money I earned working at my parent's convenience store to buy eyes I was not born with. I'd blink open into the mirror, and, after the tear-stained blur settled, there I would be: the African girl with the honey eyes.

I was caught up in the blue-eye-worshipping-mixed-race-praising culture I was surrounded by. I felt pulled in between wanting to be the Black girl who knew she had it like that and desperately wanting to fit in. I forgot that I learned to see myself in the dark first.

My first mirror was my mother's dark womb. Blackness absorbs all color until it becomes an overabundance of no-thing. We lose sight of who is who in the black of night. Femaleness, during the acts of sex and birth especially, is a blend between self and other, so close that you almost feel like you share the same muscle. And the first mirrors were black, said to originate in what is now modern-day Turkey. These mirrors were discs of obsidian polished to high shine.

Later civilizations began to use the gold, silver, and glass we are familiar with today. Among the goods traded between slavers and West African rulers for human life were: umbrellas, tobacco, fabric, guns, and mirrors. Before the advent of the transatlantic slave trade, my ancestors may have only witnessed their faces within shimmering bodies of river or ocean and each other's eyes. Once mirrors appeared, their reflections were still, clear, and black.

Our mirroring gaps, the ways we feel unseen or unwitnessed, cannot be divorced from personal and political histories. My buying of contacts occurred within a vacuum of a Eurocentric beauty ideals, Southern California vanities, and my own tender first-generation daughter anxieties. I was a vortex of longing, desperate for attention—even if that attention came from people who didn't really give a shit about me. When we receive incomplete reflections or are not witnessed fully, we tend to think there's something wrong or limiting with *us*. I had long been caught in a vague "something is wrong with me" fuzz that came from feeling at odds with so much around me. The truth was that there was nothing wrong with me. I was different, not inferior. I needed kinder mirrors.

If we were not witnessed in our joy, sadness, anger, or fear, then these emotions can become difficult to access when we are mature. We may hide our imperfections to compensate. We may ignore our less than shiny spots, ashamed to meet our complexity.[5]

---

5 An example of a complicated mirror in my Yoruba lineage is Madam Efunroye Òsuntinubu, also known as Madame Tinubu, for whom Tinubu Square in Lagos has been named. During the late nineteenth century, an era in Nigerian history where gender roles did not automatically depress a woman's chance for economic power, Madame Tinubu was an ambitious business woman—think Madame CJ Walker's business acumen—a politically astute leader, one of the first women to take a formalized recognizable stand against British colonization practices, and a woman who rose from grief (she lost her first husband and two sons) to become the Iyalode of her town, one of the most well-respected leadership designations for women in Yoruba society. Unfortunately, she also exchanged human beings for guns, positioned herself favorably in Yoruba civil wars for her singular economic benefit, and squashed the influence of formerly enslaved returnees from Sierra Leone and Brazil. Some accounts report that she later repented her slave-trading ways after hearing about the horrors

I did not become the belle of Imperial Middle School during my colored-contacts days. The skater boys I crushed on did not suddenly want to skate me home. I was more than a head taller than most of my friends, which made direct eye contact a grab bag, so there's a high chance that my friends had no idea I had even changed my eyes to Autumn Sunrise.

Part of the reason I stopped wearing colored contacts is that the insertion process hurt like a bitch. Pressing those flimsy plastic contacts against my naked eyeball skin took a very long time, stung like salt, and turned the sclera of my eyes Pedialyte pink. My body recognized those honey contacts as a foreign agent, folded its arms, and said no thank you.

When anyone or anything requires you to contort into pain and walk around with lobster eyes, it is time to ask yourself who you value more. You are free to choose a different way.

My peace with mirrors arrived when I answered truthfully *who* or *what* benefitted from my hurt. When I decided that the reflection of fake honey eyes was worth forking $20 over for, I was another investor in the billion-dollar beauty industry. While colored contacts from downtown LA are an innocuous buy, when this purchase is multiplied millions of times across the globe and across time, those honey contacts transform into a silent epidemic of Black girls and women being promised love in exchange for diluting ourselves.

We deserve more than this. We deserve to move from third-person point of view to solid first. We deserve to choose mirrors that help more than harm. We deserve to rewrite the times we origami'd ourself to fit the

---

enslaved Africans faced abroad. And some accounts say nothing of this remorse. African involvement in the transatlantic slave trade is a complicated mirror and leapfrogged over for a variety of reasons (shame, empathy triage, denial, *what will white people do with this part of the story line?* etc.). Unfortunately, the entire diaspora suffers when we decide to ignore our reflection. Yorubaland is indisputably connected to slave labor. We don't have to look very far to see how the Oyo Empire led trans-Sahara slave trading with Europeans and the Hausa or the tangled griefs of domestic servitude. Scholars bicker on the practice of slavery in Yorubaland; but the effects cannot be denied: nearly one million Yoruba people were sold as enslaved workers to the Americas between 1651 and 1867.

status quo. We are taught implicitly and explicitly that our well-being is an afterthought. Becoming my own mirror and abandoning those wounding mirrors is an embodied ownership of selfhood.

Where have you hurt yourself to appease the gaze of another? What mirrors are no longer working for your life? You deserve to see your mirroring gaps as places that are begging for your warmth and acceptance. You deserve to find the people who can see you without asking you to adjust to their reflection.

The 2019 Season 2 finale of Spike Lee's TV reboot *She's Gotta Have It* is called #IAmYourMirror. Nola Darling, the show's protagonist, is a queer polyamorous Black woman artist trying to find her way in rapidly gentrifying Brooklyn. She's pigeonholed by corporate interests who want her street cred but do not respect her spirit. The trio of hot guys she dates (nerd influencer, banker zaddy, and professional model) adore her free-love ways but mostly when she plays by their rules. Nola's recent painting is so controversial she hides it behind a heavy red curtain during her gallery show and has viewers enter the space privately.

Spoiliest of spoilers: The painting is a large-scale acrylic self-portrait of Nola being lynched by her own braids . . . naked to include pubic mons . . . draped in an American flag where the red portions resemble blood. (Subtlety is not Nola's strong suit.)

Nola's best friend Shemekka is deeply disturbed and questions Nola's right to make such art, thinking it cheapens the very real anti-Black violence she sees in her day-to-day life. Nola is stung by this rejection but stands by her right to create the art she desires—stands by the freedom to be her own mirror and linger in her own selfhood.

"Aren't I allowed to evolve?" she asks.

This is the question I ask and answer for myself now when I approach any mirror.

I am a woman now, no longer in my uncle's house.

I know what mirrors will make me bleed.

I know which mirrors keep me whole.

I once sought the ultimate impossibility: to control how others viewed me, a mini dictator, forcing the unwilling or unable to become my perfect mirror. I once thought that if I tried hard enough, I could water myself down, milk away the dark of my eyes into acceptance.

The first step in claiming your autonomy and releasing those stories that do not belong to you is to heal your relationship to seeing and being seen. You are called to become your own perfect mirror; you are called to be centered in self.

If gazing into a mirror feels approachable for you, practice looking into the mirror and telling yourself the things you most need to hear. If gazing into a mirror feels stressful, you may need to release your hold on the screens of your life: the reality dating shows, the airbrushed Instagram idealizations, the sad pits of Bumble.

Patience with your mirroring gaps is crucial.

When you gaze into the mirror, you will find your mirroring gap in the verdicts you carry, the vanities you avoid knowing, and the spaces still blurry inside.

You will find your truth.

Heather Headley plays Dr. Jamison, Nola Darling's therapist on *She's Gotta Have It*, and perpetually sounds like honey quaaludes are melting in her throat. She seems to find Nola both endearing and a bit much, and there's always some hint of a smile in her voice when she gives Nola her sure-to-be $250/hour advice. Following the fallout of her art show, Nola is faced with how to square who she is with what other people expect of her. Dr. Jamison speaks the wise, older woman words that Nola desperately needs to hear: "Individuation. It's the process required for self-actualizing. Whether you're talking about friends or family, people you admire—or despise—you have to individuate your wants from theirs in order to honor your true self. It can be a thrilling and painful process. [But] who wants to see or be a black orchid that never fully opens?"

One of Òsun's classic accessories is a mirror. She loves this thing. If you Google Òsun, there are high chances you will catch her in the stages of deep self-like, mirror in hand. Òsun is sometimes known as Òsun Yẹyẹ Moro—the mother of the mirror.[6] Òsun's mirror gazing is a grounded self-regard, where she meets her pain and pleasure simultaneously. She studies herself for herself, allowing her eyes to play and pray with what they see.

Know that when you gaze into your own eyes, you are a living Black mirror of the thousands of ancestors who made you possible; you are witnessing the abundance of possibility. You are where the world ends and begins. Your mirror gazing and your mirror healing is always for you.

Look and see for you yourself.[7]

HONEYKNIFE PRAXIS

- **Drip:** Gaze into a mirror for thirty seconds. Welcome and soften any judgment that arrives. Close your eyes whenever you need. (Mirror work can also be done in the dark.)
- **Drizzle:** For one week, compliment something you like about your body in the mirror or repeat a kind saying to your reflection.
- **Pour:** Complete a Buddhist-inspired mirror meditation and gaze upon your naked body from head to toe in a mirror for one hour straight.

---

6 Awo Fá'Lokun Fatunbi, *Oshun: Ifá and the Spirit of the River* (Original Publications, 1993).

7 "After I received Òsun, I had an earth-shaking experience. I was going to the post office, and the post office had a big plate-glass window. As I rode up to the window, I was looking at the window and I saw a woman getting off a bicycle, and I said to myself, 'She sure is pretty.' And as I walked closer I realized that the woman was me. I stood there looking with tears in my eyes." Iyalosha Majile Òsunbunmi Olafemi, interviewed by Rachel Elizabeth Harding,"What Part of the River You're In: African American Women in Devotion to Òsun." *Òsun Across the Waters: A Yoruba Goddess in Africa and the Americas,* edited by Joseph M. Murphy and Mei-Mei Sanford (Indiana University Press, 2001).

2

Slim Thick Dreams

Breathe in. Breathe out.

Welcome to your ninety-minute Bikram Yoga class, which will also serve as a qualitative study on your lingering body image issues. Today you are in Miami. About two weeks ago, you flew redeye from Pittsburgh because you have been recalled to the Coast Guard Reserves for the Hurricane Irma response. It is 2017, and you leave grad school in the smack middle of the semester, arrive in Miami in the early humid morning ready to serve your country through Excel spreadsheets and Microsoft Outlook.

You still find it tough to name your recent Florida active-duty station as a deployment. You are a sixteen-minute Uber ride from the glistening buttocks of South Beach and every other day you sample the hot food bar at Whole Foods while some of your military school classmates are on second tours in Kuwait. Your current home is a neutral brown hotel room downtown.

Your job title is Situation Unit Leader. Daily you spend hours recording the movements of oil recovery vessels, reporting up the chain-of-command, and dodging petty racism. You are lonely and your belly is a mincemeat of turbulence and bloat. Face it, you have never fully fit into the military vibe, though your father who encouraged your service academy life would have hoped otherwise. You are not a Republican or a white man and your nervous system is a tender, howling thing. You left active duty two years ago to chase your longtime writer dreams and being

29

back in your operational dress blues is a trip backwards in time to an age where every day you felt like the manifestation of that one Sesame Street jingle *one of these things is not like the other.*

Often when you feel externally displaced or anxious, your mind latches onto the supposed wrongness of your body. It is comforting to blame something so intimate to you, something so unable to argue back. And so your mind fixates on losing the same fifteen pounds, the frailty of your 4C hair, or the width of your thighs. If your body was perfect, your subconscious reasons, then you would be too.

To combat this carousel of aching thoughts, you decide to go to hot yoga after another Coastie suggests a nearby studio. You know the founder of Bikram Yoga is a tyrant and sexual pervert who is still somehow certifying instructors in Mexico. You wish yoga could stop being so basic, but alas, misuses of power will find any vehicle, even ones that promote mindbodysoul peace. You also know that Bikram Yoga is a sequence of twenty-six poses in a 105-degree room with 40% humidity for one hour and a half that allows the worst of your inner critic to subside and makes your fascia feel brand new.

Leaving your hotel room, you stuff a bleached towel in your backpack and fill up your eco-friendly water jug in the hallway. The Brickell Bridge carries you across the Miami River, from the skid row sidewalks towards the financial center of Miami and Saks Fifth Avenue. Each time you cross this expanse you marvel at the thin line connecting such economically disparate worlds. *This is a metaphor,* you think, but you are too intent on the Drake song preaching about haters and Biscayne in your earbuds to dwell any deeper.

You find the studio.

You are delighted: the room does not reek of sweaty feet.

Breathe in. And out.

It is time for the first yoga position, Half-Moon.

A gentle lean to the right and left imitates the shifting crescent.

You are wearing teal lipstick and booty shorts in black; your locs are pulled up into mid-ponytail. Bending down, hands to feet, you notice another woman enter the barely lit studio. The energy in the room cyclones towards her. *What is so special about her?* you jealously think and then quickly censure your displeasure with feminist goodwill. You want to take your kindness all the way back when you witness the source of the magnetic drag that grabbed the studio's attention as she turns to the right. Her ass is colossal, a Jungian shadow, a planetary achievement clad in premium Lululemon spandex.

Breathe in. And out.

Maybe her ass is fake? Sinking down to your mat into Awkward Pose, you realize your women's rights affirmations will not soothe this new ache that has slapped your ass envy awake. You have way less ass than this woman beside you. This is Miami, where contestants from *Love and Hip Hop* dine at the same riverfront Greek restaurant, where you finally learn where all those bodycon Fashion Nova outfits are worn in analog life. Beauty in Miami is an extreme sport taken more seriously than in your native SoCal, a fact you never thought possible.

In your native Orange County, curves were generally seen as trouble. You grew up with the angular shoulders of Jennifer Aniston and Britney Spear's jutting hip bones. White girls complained about their asses getting too big during second period, and overhearing them, you wondered if you were having a *Twilight Zone* moment. An ass that was *too large?* You didn't understand how ass could ever be excessive, let alone a problem.

But the tides changed after Jennifer Lopez, Shakira and her honest hips, and the visual assault of Instagram. Finally, white girls discovered the charm of prominent gluteals, digested the message that every Black and Brown girl with a flat behind received upon puberty: that ass was plus rather than demerit. Fashion standard *Vogue*, a magazine primarily known for celebrating emaciated models from Belarus, declared 2014 the Year of the Booty. Much in the same manner that actress Bo Derek made beaded braids adorably chic in the late 1970s, women who are not Black have benefitted the most from this relatively new ass-positive mainstream landscape. Though the thighs often do not match and you feel sorry for whatever has happened to Madonna's backside, the consensus had finally shifted for the white mainstream: ass was cool and good to have.

The Bikram ass you are witnessing should star in its own park bench ad. This woman's ass is pert and balloon-like, no cellulite indents, no sag, no disproportion, not a squarish edge to be found, like an angel in butt form rescued straight out of an early 2000s music video. *It's not real*, you repeat to yourself like you're rolling on ketamine and trying to calm down.

That ass cannot, should not, be real.

Breathe out. And in.

But what if it is real? you wonder as you wobble into Eagle Pose.

By now, your skin is glistening with sweat, the hot salt racing into your eyes, discoloring your aging sports bra. The Bikram ass belongs to a short white woman, maybe Latina, close to middle-age. Do not lie—it makes you sorta sad to know that white girls with bigger asses than you exist. *Like, it's not enough to colonize the world and leech the marrow from affirmative action, it's not enough to colonize yoga and TikTok, now you want ass too?* You had a white friend in high school who all the Black guys lusted after with open abandon. Sarah with the Big Ass was her creative nickname. The attention she received sometimes made you feel bad about yourself. She did not like her ass exactly, often resorted to covering it with long sweatshirts and baggy jeans. To you, it was like throwing a wet blanket over a silver Bentley.

Once, you asked a boyfriend if you had a big butt. He looked at you with sweet pity, and said, "I mean for a white girl, you're good, but for a Black girl—" You pushed your fingers to his lips. "Don't finish that sentence," you interjected before he caused you to slip into depression. You breathe in the tea tree oil-scented air and try not to think about your body image.

Breathe in. Breathe out.

Of course, this means that you *are* thinking about your body image. You desire physical perfection in one breath, correct yourself for this vapid desire in the next. How have you still not outgrown this desire about the power of pretty?

There is an almost universal belief that Black women uniformly love our bodies.[8] That we are a horde of confidence who never dream of Botox on our lunch breaks. You remember pitching a magazine article on the nuance of Black woman body image once: The blonde editor's eyebrows wrinkle into a performance art called bewilderment the longer you speak. "But, I thought Black women liked being, you know, fat?" she finally asks.

You hide your sigh because you really want the byline and the money. You tell her how those surveys in question position the skinny ideal as the only prerequisite for body image struggles. You tell her that 90% of all women regardless of gender, age, and racial background cite their body as a high cause of shame.[9] You tell her that even though Black women rarely aim for ectomorphic proportions, that Black body image standards are often even *more* exacting.[10] A pretty Black woman should be: thick, but not *too* thick and only in the ass and hips and butts and occasional thighs; racially ambiguous; and, if your parents did not mix well enough to be octoroons, at least have the decency to be light-skinned. You don't delve into the complex storyline that is Black woman and hair because your blonde editor would probably ask so many questions about weaves that you would become resentful.

You tell her that Black women are socialized to never admit defeat, even on anonymous surveys. The editor nods and passes you a recently published essay: a white coed who struggled over the space of 2,500 words

---

8 "'Strong Black Women,' we are taught, are a monolith of pear-shaped, curvy, sashaying, devil-may-care neck rollers . . . Countless body satisfaction studies use white women as the control group, consequently focusing on weight and ignoring skin tone and hair texture. The skewed result is that Black women seem more self-assured, lending clinical credence to our unwritten cultural rules. Perhaps the stereotype would be positive if it were true. But we are human. Whether we admit it or not, we, too, internalize unattainable beauty standards and hold warped notions of the purpose of our bodies." (Bird and Solomon, 2005)

9 Brene Brown, *The Gifts of Imperfection* (Hazelden Publishing, 2010).

10 Byrd, Ayana D., and Akiba Solomon. *Naked: Black Women Bare All about Their Skin, Hair, Hips, Lips, and Other Parts.* Perigee, 2005.

with how much foundation to wear to the office.

"She could teach you something," the editor says.

Breathe in. And out.

Balancing towards a semblance of Standing Bow, you remind yourself not to believe the Instagram, slow-motion hype.

All asses are good asses, right?

Part of you is ashamed that you are even having these thoughts in the first place. You are a feminist who read Audre Lorde and bell hooks for funsies. You go to therapy! You should not be so fixated on outward beauty. You agonize over disappointing some invisible Body Positive Police.[11] You invent hashtags in your mind, trying not to stare at Bikram Ass.

#AssAcceptance.

Slogans and captions would read: All asses matter! Your ass is good enough! Your ass is perfectly divine and worthy of unretouched capture!

But you do not *know.* Maybe if you worked just a little harder on those slow squats? Who knows what magic would occur?!

Breathe in. And out..

Your hands reach towards the air in front in Balancing Stick.

Your mind flutters with futuristic excitement as a montage builds in your mind.

Just imagine *you* and all that ass.

How *unstoppable* you would be.

You are sauntering down the street in silk and see-through jersey. You are entering glittering parties backwards, posing in natural light with hand on hip, a hundred naughty winks in your eye. You marry an intellectual millionaire. You wear sequined thongs around your house and balance Coke cans at the curvature of your spine. Your ass becomes your

---

11 Sonya Renee Taylor's wonderful book, *The Body Is Not an Apology,* offers a compassionate gaze towards the complicated feelings we have towards our bodies, that stubborn shame of our shame: "Avoid meta-shame for having so much shame. Take a deep breath of kindness for yourself and your history of body shame/shaming. We can only do what we know. As famed poet Maya Angelou says, 'When we know better, we do better.' We can do better by giving ourselves more love."

hallmark. You are feminine embodiment and work 85% less on twerking (because let's face it, little booties have to work harder). Oh, the songs that rhapsodize when you strut down avenues, the sunflower bouquets, the Spanish style mansions!

Breathe in. And out.

Standing Separate Leg Pose. Triangle. Head to Knee. Tree Pose.

You wipe your face and big ass fantasies away with a small hand towel.

You won't be attempting Toe Stand Pose tonight—you are exhausted.

You are now in Dead Body Pose, and your thoughts continue to swim as you bring your left knee up for Wind Relief Pose. And it is in this fart-releasing asana that you wonder with warm tenderness what would happen if you quit this whole game of wanting to be someone you are not? If you loved the as-is of your body with as much grace as you could.

Breathe in. Breathe out.

From the ages of ten to eighteen, you wanted to be a model. You can be forgiven for this wild card dream: you are a California-bred millennial with early childhood trauma and a talent for escapist fantasy. You researched the industry via a book you bought with your own birthday money—*The Modeling Life*, by Donna Rubenstein.

Donna is frank and informative—if you are a young woman who has not been discovered by a photographer at LAX or lounging on Virginia Beach by age fourteen, chances are high you will never strut down Milan runways. Before *America's Next Top Model* comes through, you are a teenager with thorough knowledge of proper go-see attire, headshot requirements, and the differences between print and catalog.

You want to be a model because models are ambassadors of beauty who grace magazines and contort into the emotions you dream of exuding: easy confidence, ferocity, studied nonchalance. You want to be a model because you believe this title will grant you the surety you need to believe in your own beauty. You want to be a model because you want to be discovered, a diamond in the rough, rescued from your tepid suburban existence into a Balenciaga-adorned future. You seem to forget that the modeling life is a cutthroat industry littered with diet pill addiction, champagne diets, anorexia, and chronic sexual harassment, where even supermodels are put out to pasture by twenty-five, and that 90% of the time you don't like how you look in photos.

Your favorite models are Naomi Campbell, Grace Jones, Farida Khelfa, Aisha Cain—all Black women or women of color who revolutionized the runway. You watch *This Model's Life* on E! and practice your smize in any mirror that will have you. You only order dry ass salads when you go to Carl's Jr. Your parents are kind towards your aspirations. You are twelve, thirteen, fourteen. They drive you and your sister from Orange County to Santa Monica two times for talent calls you find in the newspaper, the back of a magazine.

You have already memorized your flaws: dimensions beyond the typical 36-24-36 requirements, acne scars, and a slight belly pooch. At over six feet, you are in fact *too* tall.

But still, you go.

Donna Rubenstein has warned you—places that ask for money are probably not agencies. It is the year 2000, home of Y2K and sadistic low-rise jeans. You have sights set on Wilhelmina, Elite, IMG. This California Barbizon, a modeling and acting school headquartered in Tampa, Florida, with satellite locations all over America, that advertised the same black-and-white ad in the back pages of young adult magazines like *YM* and *Teen*, is a stepping stone. One day, you hope to laugh about your humble beginnings at a dinner party as Ryan Gosling winks across the table.

At your last and final audition, you walk down a short hotel runway, hoping you appear as a doppelgänger of Naomi's sure sashay. You read a commercial script about cookies and milk. The panel regards you with cool eyes.

A dreadlocked, brown-skinned man scores you: *You slur your words, and you need to work on your figure.* Miraculously, you never become bulimic or mute in response, but his words ring in your head for long years: every time you speak, every time you bring something sugary to your mouth. You make one last half-hearted attempt to send your pictures to *America's Next Top Model* during your first year at prep military school in New Mexico.

Your budding photographer friend takes the photos with a disposable Kodak.

When the photos return, you see a sad-eyed girl with hair sporting split ends from too many Dark & Lovely relaxers.

You do not send the photos.

The modeling life is not for you.

Breathe in. And out.

When you were not fantasizing about embodying the androgynous figure of a high fashion model, you wanted to be Girl with Curves. You know which body the basketball boys you crush on worship at the altar of.[12] You know what body produces cartoonish slack-jaw effect: that guitar-like hip-to-waist ratio, hefty Blade Runner thighs, and somehow always a flat belly. This is the dizzying aspect of your body image story: how quickly your insecurities shift depending on your latitude and longitude, who liked a picture of you eating gelato, the sparkling abs of the Newest Batch of It Girl.

You wonder if there is one singular body that would satisfy the competing demands of your life. You are a social nomad, traveling between the tribes of thick-praising Black girls, girls of color who wore shapewear like insurance, and white girls who thirsted after the jutting hip bones of messy era Britney Spears. In the Coast Guard, you were placed

---

12 Phatness, an affirmative declaration I only heard utilized in 1990s movies, perfectly described the music video starlets of a certain era. Before the current batch of Instagram Baddies were even born, the video vixen was the reigning representation of Black and Brown woman sexiness. (She counts the *Jet* Beauty of the Week and pin-up girls as her predecessors.) In early music videos, everyday Black girls in varying tones and body shapes danced in the background. As rap became more mainstream, video vixens rapidly replaced "round the way girls," and established the visual conformity we know today: lighter-skinned, hour-glass bodies with lengthy weaves or "Spanish" hair. Video vixens were desired and reviled in equal measure, subject to erotic jealousy and wanton disrespect without a #metoo reckoning. Some of these video vixens, like Melyssa Ford and Karrine Steffans, became household names. Most others remained nameless, unknown.

on probation for weighing over standards. The process was affectionately called "the fat boy program."

You would be better off having more than one body, a closet of options: one body for the 10:00 a.m. worship service at your uncle's Apostolic church; one body for lunch meetings with the white supervisor who subsists on unseasoned chicken breasts; one body that pleases aunties during Christmas dinner; one body for Tinder dates in Italy; another body for "free before 11:00" at a Sunset Boulevard lounge.

Breathe in. And out.

By now, your shorts are completely drenched and stuck to your medium- (one can hope) sized behind. The class moves from head to knee to stretching: Spine Twisting Pose. The teacher's Bikram bark calms down to slow and easy as the class shifts into Kapalbhati, shallow breathing exercises.

For some moments, your mind drifts away from the comparison, relaxes into the present. This is what you love about yoga the most: the way your mind, spirit, and body unionize into one dewy song. After class you take a quick shower and throw your wet clothes into your backpack, where they dye the dark purple fabric almost black.

You emerge into the sticky Miami air feeling supple and alive.

You visit that hot yoga studio twice a week for the remainder of your time in Miami, but you never see that woman and her Bikram ass again.

Breathe in. And out.

Weeks later, you have completed your reserve duty and have been de-activated from the Hurricane Irma response. You are back in Pittsburgh, ready to resume graduate classes. You are trying to mold your sporadic LA Fitness jaunts into something resembling routine and not rushed exertions where you spend the majority of your workout time wallowing in your Camry and descending into Wikipedia rabbit holes about the cast of *Freaks and Geeks*. You mostly work out in the Women's Only gym space on the lower level, a mirrored room replete with one elliptical, a handful of weight machines, and baby dumbbells in tropical colors.

You love this room because it is small and private, away from the macho classic rock of the main floor. Usually, there is one woman performing crunches on the floor, another breezily jogging on the treadmill. And sometimes, you watch *Sex and the City* reruns while performing your squats.

You are on one of the beat-up mats on the floor, when in walks a woman who would grace *King* magazine if print media wasn't disappearing like Bay Area real estate. She is wearing a baseball cap pulled down low and a matching pastel, high-waisted compression set.

Her butt is so big it appears to speak as she takes her place on the elliptical.

Don't mind me, just bouncing my life away!

Why are you wasting time doing crunches when it is obvious you should be chained to a Stair Master? you think to yourself. *Did you think this woman and her LA Fitness booty did lazy cardio sets and won the day?* Before you venture too deep down a live action compare and contrast essay about your flaws, the Ghost of Bikram Booty twerks around the fitness room, prompting you to choose anew.

C'mon, girl, again? Ghost of Bikram Booty asks. *Is this really the road you want to go down?*

Breathe in. Breathe out.

You do not have body image insecurities because you are vain or stupid or weak.

You live in a world where the Black woman body is both desired and vilified, persecuted and worshipped. You live in a space where bodies are cursed lifeless carriers taking second place to the spirit. You live in a Westernized expanse where thinness is the ticket of admission to elite circles (fine art, country clubs, assumed intelligence), actively diffusing the closed doors attached to race, color, or class. Thinness is equated to discipline, intellect, and control, a carefully maintained artificial reality. Collegiate influencers are investing in lip fillers, and every other week a woman loses her life to a Brazilian butt lift.

Beauty is a wild world, rife with casualties.

You have been sold the idea that your perceived attractiveness matters more than your character, your passions, your spirit since you were knee-high. It's like, *"I know she saved the Apollo mission, but is she hot?"* How many times have you witnessed the overt improvement in how a woman is regarded from a superficial change: a weave, contact lenses, losing ten pounds?

While you love the rise of "body positivity," you recognize there are significant limits to a movement so deeply tied to digital performance and mainstream capitalism. Body positivity owes its rabid rise to the blogging heyday of the early aughts and the work of fat lesbians of color, and you are grateful for the realistic, non-air-brushed bodies you now witness on the daily. There are still unspoken rules: plus-size models with flat bellies, small facial features, and tight jawlines, celebrities constantly advertising their muscled postpartum bodies, skinny teas, and elaborate skin care rituals.

As a teenager, you were a voracious reader of magazines that clearly messed up some aspects of your mental health around realistic body expectations, but at least you could put the *Seventeen* down and close the pages of *CosmoGirl*. Today your own stylized and filtered peers serve as comparison, and plastic surgery is treated like routine self-care. Real lives have become the magazines you desired to emulate from afar.

There is no one body that promises a pain-free life; you know this, even when the propaganda suggests otherwise. Underneath the distracting thoughts, the obsessive comparison, the worries about your belly fat is a vast reservoir of unclaimed desire. Skinny is a *feeling* you have chased for years, without resolution no matter how slender or well-toned you became. You are not alone. How else to explain that women who are size 0 or who are size 16 embody the same panic about not being skinny enough?

Your chase for the "perfect body" had little to do with perfection, fat, or even the body. When you got honest about all the things you were putting off doing until "my body is good enough," you realized how much you were depending on your body to protect you from external harm both real and imaginary. Skinny is safety from the casual cruelty of unevolved men. Skinny is easy access to the fine art world. Skinny is being offered more money for an editorial job. Skinny is more swipes on Bumble. Skinny is beautiful clothes that aren't boxy kaftans. Skinny is no one saying anything when you ask for another helping of jollof rice.

Body positivity places a lot of pressure on women to always have love for our bodies, which, in such a body-disrespecting culture as ours, is not only unrealistic but also pretty fucking mean. When you are clear about what your Perfect Body is a stand-in for, you flow into the more accessible body neutrality, a practice of coming to peace with what your unmet needs and desires are, but also the present experience of your body—whether you think you're hot or not, whether you go on that paleo cleanse or eat carbs without guilt.

Breathe in. And out.

"How you meet your yoga mat is how you meet your life" is a quote you've heard from every yoga instructor worth her 200-hour certification. These are also words you rolled your eyes at. *How didactic,* you think. *How tedious.* And yet there you would be in almost every one-hour class, pushing and pulling your limbs from one pose to the next, intent on becoming fluidity in motion. You saw props like bolsters and rolled up mats as defeat. Over the years, your ego-based desire has calmed down enough for you to realize the futility of your striving: all these years of battling, and you still cannot unbend your knees in Downward Dog. And so, stubborn at first, then shyly eager, you meet your tight hamstrings and your desires for perfection where they are.

Your beauty story is another untangling, a way to meet your relationship to beauty as she is, relaxing the hardened places. You meet that tender yearning for beauty as your desire for love.

Most days, you know you're cute, but let's be real: you will never be Bonita Applebaum or Ms. Fat Booty: The Sequel. You will not be discovered in a crowded supermarket and spirited away to Paris Fashion

Week. Social media will probably morph beauty into more exacting strangeness as plastic surgery becomes mundane and virtual reality allows ordinary humans to reach the outward perfection of demigods. Thinness will continue to be a calling card for sophistication in many circles, and the world will continue its slow, jagged march to a reality where all bodies are valued just as they are.

Your body will enter new gravities and transform.

You probably won't be *ecstatic* about every one of these changes, no matter how much Sonya Renee Taylor or Black feminist texts you read.

It is okay to grieve the perfect body you wanted and still desire even now.

And it's okay to behold the beauty of who you are.

In the mirror, you take note of all 75-inches of you, the delicate curves of muscle and dark skin. You leave the LA Fitness room, and the clang of dropping barbells meets you.

You decide to walk like a woman with a big ass.

In this moment, full of breath, even with your unconscious probably still deducing the price of Ozempic and a butt lift, you strut down an aisle of empty grey treadmills. It is tenuously delicious to walk as if beauty, the love you wanted all your life, has already been found.

When you were seven years old, you believed you were beautiful because you had a small spherical dot above your upper lip. A beauty mark. And because Marilyn Monroe, Janet Jackson, and Cindy Crawford had one, you believed with easy devotion that you were part of the beautiful club. Today, faintly sweaty with your gym bag over your shoulder, you feel free, peaceful even. A cloud has departed your aura, and you do not care if anyone else confirms your beauty; for this small moment, much like when you were seven, beauty is yours.

You will forget this permission to decide your worth outside of beauty of course. You will get caught up in wishing and shrinking. You may attempt to outsource this decision to a man's eyes or some decaying ideal still stuck in the shadow of your brain.

Then, you will remember why you forgot this permission.

And then you will try again.

Slow breath in. Slow breath out.

Welcome to your practice.

Welcome to your body.

HONEYKNIFE PRAXIS

- **Drip:** Make a list of all the good things your body can do—bear hugs, heartbeats, hiking, tasting, orgasming—and read it often, especially on more sensitive days.
- **Drizzle:** Go on a media diet for a month and only digest media that helps you feel chill or happy about your present body. How did it feel?
- **Pour:** Start a yoga practice that makes you feel good.

3

To All the Dark-Skinned Girls I Was Before

I really do not want to tell another Sad Dark-Skinned Girl Story, but I have one in my back pocket should any artist grant require it.

I am around eight years old. I am in my room, towel wrapped, just out of the bath, squeezing the last remaining drops from a bottle of Crème of Essence—a body lotion containing hydroquinone, a depigmenting agent that in large quantities murders melanin into fairness. I always thought Crème of Essence and other bleaching cremes smelled like caged farts, and yet I smoothed it on my girl skin, entertaining some floating feather fantasy of transforming into Raven-Symoné, reigning light-skinned protagonist of my early years.

The Sad Dark-Skinned Girl has been made famous in single-issue documentaries and social media campaigns where she begs emotionally stunted rappers for a music video cameo. *I'm pretty too!* While the Tragic Mulatto Myth romanticizes light-skinned or biracial women as self-destructive sirens intent on creating social havoc (see early cinema like *Pinky* and *Imitation of Life* and the more recent *The Vanishing Half* for examples of this trope; read work by Nella Larsen for counterbalance), the Sad Dark-Skinned Girl is violence in pigtails.

Devalued by her melanotic brethren, rejected by a color-struck society, and reduced to the pigment of her skin, she (and so often, the figure in this trope is a "she"; a supposed loss of beauty is equated to the ultimate feminine curse) is destined to wander the earth considering Clorox baths. She is a bitter cartoon who loves nothing more than to hate herself, slice off the bouncy curls of mixed-race-girl hair, and spend precious protagonist energy being kicked around chapter to chapter. Her main inward lament a repeating refrain of disgust that she is not Marilyn Monroe.

I was never Pecola Breedlove, little girl heroine of Toni Morrison's debut novel *The Bluest Eye*, lusting after eyes of cerulean. I can't lie and say I didn't envy the careful attention little white girls received or that I have never coveted the generous benefit of doubt gifted towards white women, but at no point in my life did I ever desire to be white.

There was, however, a certain shade of Black girl I desired to look like once upon a time: light-skinned and chirpy, with impeccable styled Just-for-Me curls or a wild mane of coils. She had hazel eyes that teachers complimented. Black boys adored this girl for what she brought to their social status, masturbated to the *blanquimento* potential for their gene pool. Darker-skinned girls offered themselves as her personal ladies-in-waiting. Media narratives entertained a caressing pity for light-skinned girls, visibly torn between the white and Black worlds, fiercely envied, so *misunderstood*.

If I were light, I would be allowed a complex sensitivity. If I were light, I might be cast as beauty queen or the pretty girl in my real life. If I were light, people would ask me where I was really from and care to hear the answer.

In elementary school, I cried over the vague hostilities about my dark skin, the nighttime jokes, the intrusive questions about the color of my gums. In junior high, I transformed secondary school tears into bad poetry about romantic rejection. In high school, I watched my long-term crush—a point guard with ridiculous dimples whom I and a friend nicknamed "Sexual Chocolate" within our gel-pen letters to each other—ask my light-skinned friend to Homecoming and she said yes.

Military school provided some relief from colorism; at the time of my graduation in 2009, there were three Black women in the entire regiment and paper bag tests were the least of our concerns. I noticed there was still a stubborn insistence in professional and personal circles that light skin was synonymous with "handle with care," but bringing up this topic often inflamed tempers and the discussion would regress into a #TeamDark-Skinned versus #TeamLightSkinned debate. I learned it was better to be quiet, to say nothing.

I know the reception of dark skin has changed dramatically over the decades. While color is still a volatile subject, today dark skin is in vogue, literally and figuratively. In 2019, four obviously Black women were pageant queens from the national to the universal stage. Thanks to a saturation of social media images and the kingdom of Wakanda, dark-skinned women control the narrative. We show off our enviable qualities: the sheen, the attractive contrast to high tone colors, the gorgeous span of our deep dark brown.

On television, dark-skinned women are playing more than the long-suffering mammy figure or the sarcastic shrew with an attitude problem. We are the girls next door, the romantic leads, the smarty pants. We are called beautiful because of our skin not in spite of it. This expansion of beauty is a welcome rebalance to the way dark skin was treated in the past, but one rarely heals from any -ism through The Media. It would be like placing a Band-Aid on a magazine.

I wonder how much these onscreen presentations overlap with the Real Life experiences of hiring interviews, family nicknames, and sorority picks. If Spotify rappers weren't going to get called out for colorism, would they really cast a dark-skinned model as their love interest? Perhaps. But perhaps they also were intelligent to understand the politics of visual representation. Advertising loves nothing more than a wound, and it is pretty suspect that the same system that perpetuated the pain of invisibility now offers itself as cure.

The medicine of public recognition is a placebo for the healing we dark-skinned girls and women really need. We lose sight of the bigger picture when we overvalue and overly depend on unrealities to make us feel good. We deserve more than the Sad Dark-Skinned tropes that leech complexity from our stories. We deserve a layered healing that acknowledges the complexity of our hurt *and* our anger. We deserve love outside of social media campaigns and a way to speak about the personal fallout from a political system.

Today, I love my dark skin like the tongue in my mouth, an adoration so unconscious I almost forget it is there. I could tell you that my appreciation of my dark skin, my African face, was cemented via Frantz Fanon and India Arie, and they undoubtedly boosted my confidence, but what brought me to true gratitude was a willingness to go deeper than simplistic Sad Dark-Skinned Girl stories, an honest process of meeting and forgiving all the dark-skinned girls I was before.

My favorite definition of forgiveness comes from a book I bought for $1.99 cents: *Forgiveness*.[13] I visit thrift stores with my mom and sister, and the Wednesday I bought forgiveness was a green-tag sale—half off. The book was unapologetically 1990s, the title in red script, and inside there were detailed exercises on how to move through forgiveness without all that flattening "just let it go" toxic positivity BS.

Previously, I had defined forgiveness as turning the other cheek, stoically ignoring the terrible "What Would Jesus Do?" and all that jazz. Forgiveness meant forgetting, condoning—a binary vacillation between punitive humiliation and selfish permissiveness. But in this book, forgiveness is a blending of seven stages: denial, self-blame, anger, victim, indignation, survivor, and integration. Real-life forgiveness contains an assortment of emotions beyond neatly defined stages; these phases are helpful borders that describe the messy process of forgiveness.

While the stages of forgiveness follow a decidedly nonlinear path, Dark-Skinned Girl as Denial is usually the first stop. Denial is a willful or accidental ignorance—a belief that if we ignore our pain, it will

---

13 Sidney B. Simon and Suzanne Simon, *Forgiveness: How to Make Peace With Your Past and Get on With Your Life* (New York: Grand Central Publishing, 1991).

magically disappear. But sometimes denial is how we save our soul. There were the internet jerks instructing dark-skinned women not to wear red lipstick, the "freedom fighters" whose girlfriends almost always looked like Black girls dipped in vanilla, and the casual way darkness was equated with adorable things like moral depravity, terror, and depression. I tried to ignore my aunties throwing money to the almost $5-billion global bleaching industry, the aunties who risked skin cancer to stand out in a sea of various browns.[14]

Have you ever *tried to ignore* something? It'd be like asking you not to think of a pink elephant. We try denial because there are few who can hold space for our particular pain. Insecurity was the province of white girls with too much time on their hands.

Alas, denial does not work because denial is a lie. I *was* hurt by these obvious displays of colorism. I *did* feel a certain kind of way whenever I heard "pretty for a dark-skinned girl." Through implicit and explicit demonstration, these people and their behaviors were teaching me that my dark skin was inherently worth less than lightness. Denial only exists because there is something that cannot be faced. And so, my Dark-Skinned Girl as Denial festered until she erupted into bitter complaint.

Enter Dark-Skinned Girl as Impressive Victim. I was *rea-dy*. Armed to the *teeth* with personal anecdotes (all those high school dances!), academic theory, and qualitative music video theory. No one wants to be victim, even actual victims. For those of us who have been rewarded for silencing our pain, the victim stage allows the space to admit hurt. I was finally heard in my sadness, annoyance, anger, and grief. Acknowledging the ways we have been victimized is a necessary stage of forgiveness that Black women are often ushered out of prematurely.

I had to acknowledge my hurt. I owned the ways narrow beauty ideals affected my romantic self-concept. While denying the pain made me

---

14 Swaminathan Natarajan, "Women wey dey use dangerous 'skin-lightening products' dey risk dia health," *BBC World Service*, July 7, 2019.

somewhat of a G, a haughty first Aunt Viv who knew her worth, speaking my pain aloud in the language of victimhood put me in the league with the Emma Lou Morgans of the world, the reigning SSD of the literary imagination.

Emma Lou Morgan is the primary character in *The Blacker the Berry*, a 1929 novel by Wallace Thurman that is considered one of the first novels to address color prejudice. Other notable dark-skinned literary heroines include: Tangy Mae Quinn in *The Darkest Child* by Delores Phillips; and Pecola Breedlove, *The Bluest Eye*, and Lula Ann Bridewell, *God Help the Child*, both by Toni Morrison. Staying too long in Victim means I bypassed my agency, my ability to, at the very least, take a multi-faceted view of my experience.

In Victim, I ignored evidence that complicated my worldview of darkness as victim. After all, there were people who did see me, people who appreciated dark skin without fetish. While I have encountered un-apologetic colorists waxing on about *preferences*, I have also dated many men who were more than appreciative of how I looked; I've been on the receiving end of many compliments. When I was in Victim mode, my views became a tunnel vision attuned to rejection. It was a clever way to avoid intimacy. If I believed I was going to be refused anyways, why bother opening up?

Witness entry of Dark-Skinned Girl as Self-Blame. Sometimes, I felt ashamed of my grief, embarrassed even. One of the surreal moments of my dark-skinned girlworld is meeting other dark-skinned women who seldom experienced colorism. Thankfully, unlike unicorns, dark-skinned girls who like their skin *do* exist. There are dark-skinned girls who matured in majority Black places where their beauty was affirmed, dark girls with parents who bought them chocolate Cabbage Patch dolls. Some dark-skinned girls just knew, marrow deep and sure, that the shade of their skin was pretty—or at the very least, a neutral feature lacking colonized charge.

If victimhood is perpetually pointing the finger outward, Dark-Skinned Girl as Self-Blame is condemning the self for feeling. Dark-skinned girls who did not feel the sting of colorism were not a negative for me—they were an alternative to the self-protecting reality I was living. To transition from self-blame, I didn't need to bury my grief under a rock. I needed an extroversion of my sadness—I needed to get mad.

Observe Dark-Skinned Girl Indignation. I wanted lighter-skinned women to feel the sting of exclusion. I was irate at light-skinned favor and deeply annoyed that light skin magically meant moral decency.[15] My anger was sometimes even arrogance; most days I did indeed think I was pretty. I always found it odd when people would gloat about the presence of European or "Indian" blood in their familial lines, willfully ignorant to the not-so-ancient sexual violence that most likely produced their wavy hair and green eyes. Sometimes I took my dark skin, high cheekbones, and full lips as evidence of my "purity," a visual testimony that I was the definition of Indigenous African beauty, of Africa, of the beginning of the world itself.

Anger reclaimed a sense of self-ownership. When I was angry, I was acknowledging my self-worth; I was taking back my power to name my experience for what it was. I was no longer being knocked over and out by sadness. The cost to being reduced to my anger was that I was not very nice and was fast becoming *more* like the people I couldn't stand. Light-skinned girls were simply playing the cards they were dealt. Did I truly know who I would have been if I had had Rihanna's hazel eyes or Meghan Markle's fair skin?

My anger reflected my unhealthy relationship to beauty. I deeply believed in the folklore of attractiveness: that female prettiness opened doors and granted a comfortable seat at the table. Real life is achingly more complicated. While light-skinned women do benefit from a mythology that

---

15 Most of light-skinned/dark-skinned discussions hug the borders of romance and desirability when colorism has far more wide-reaching effects. In one prison study, lighter skinned women were given more forgiving incarceration sentences and spent less time behind bars overall. Our criminal justice system is a legacy of social ills; colorism is just one sad part (Jil Viglione, Lance Hannon, and Robert DeFina, "The Impact of Light Skin on Prison Time for Black Female Offenders," *The Social Science Journal*, 48.1, 250–58, January 2011).

imbues beauty, sexual desirability, and worth (please spare me the idea that Leslie Jones and Rashida Jones have the same Black woman experience), they, like the pitied Spitefully Sad Dark-Skinned Girl, are still living within a shaky misconception, a social lie that ultimately serves whiteness. I have light-skinned friends who felt like little else besides a trophy. I know of light women sidelined in the modern-day dating circuit for someone even lighter and brighter than they. Many light-skinned people, though they may reap advantages due to colorism, are deeply uncomfortable with a hierarchy they did not create.

Some scholars have attributed the favor shown to lighter-skinned children as a survival strategy for enslaved, colonized Black women. In the "New World," the majority of these first light-skinned children were birthed from rape. Some say these mothers loved their light-skinned children harder to soften the pain of their conception.[16]

My empathy towards lighter-skinned people has changed, especially as I reflect on my dark-skin advantages: dark skin as a more recognizable portrait of native Black beauty, visual Blackness as unambiguous (rarely does a stranger ask me where I'm *really* from), skin imbued with natural sun protection factor that is twice the amount of lighter skin. These are good things.

Dark-skinned woman can birth a rainbow; our children can be violet-tinged black to alabaster white. I have seen Grace Jones's granddaughter, and I know that I could have a light-skinned daughter one day. I would want her to love all of who she was. A lighter-skinned girl who owns her beauty is only a threat to the degree that I have not held my own pain, so I commit to moving beyond reactive resentment. Admittedly, I am not the best woman for a light-skinned woman to vent her *all-the-dark-Black-girls-hated-me-because-the-boys-loved-me* lament. However deep my empathy, I have very little desire to serve as the doula of light-skinned

---

16 bell hooks, *Rock My Soul: Black People and Self-Esteem* (New York: Washington Square Press, 2004).

esteem this lifetime. I accept the unfinished business of all the dark-skinned girls I was before, what they desire and what they resist. They are a knowing contingent, every emotion a clue.

What we humans do with darkness is weird, to say the least. We have made a simple trait determined by the MC1R gene into a symbol burdened by tacky beliefs and lazy assumptions. Albinism is treated in vastly disparate ways across the African continent, from lucky feature to outright curse. Some color-based caste systems actually *predate* white supremacy. Light skin mania decorates too much of our earth. Maybe humans fear the power of darkness so much they project their anxieties onto the humans who remind them of night, earth, and shadow. Maybe lighter-skinned humans who typically do not fare well with UV rays wish to ensure the survival of their recessive genes and create a permanent working-class caste, an eternal fieldhand, easily identified by the rich dark of their skin. Who knows. What I do know is that dark skin deserves much better than this, and I refuse to to carry the weight of ignorant cruelties.

Dark-Skin Girl as Survivor and Dark-Skin Girl as Integration accepts the color-struck world she lives in and chooses her own definitions, knowing this choice is affected by her environment. Dark-skinned girls have survived loneliness, uninformed comments, death by bleaching, the paper bag test. In this stage of forgiveness, I realized I am more than the stories assigned to the dark. I can be soft with my darkness. I can relax into my darkness. I thank the social theorists, lay scholars, and deep-thinking friends who taught, healed, and listened to me. I thank my Pan-African-ish upbringing, Lauryn Hill, and that one gymnastic girl in *The Lost World: Jurassic Park* movie for being the stepping stool towards my own self-regard.

I forgive not to course correct history or even to protest; I forgive because I want to be free. I do not forgive those who have not taken accountability for how their colorist actions affect dark-skinned people. I do not forgive the creators and upholders of color caste systems who show zero remorse for their actions. I do not forgive mean-spirited people who have never apologized for the carelessness of their words. I do not forgive a society too lazy and unwilling to notice dark beauty.

Here's my Dark-Skinned Girl Story again.

Warning, it ends well.

The day I was about to rub that Crème of Essence onto my eight-year-old skin, my father found me, oily dollop in the center of my palm. He took the bottle and, in a voice lacking any meanness, told me to never use such a thing again. And I never did. I remember his hands, the smooth skin of a watertight drum.

Your dark-skinned girl forgiveness is about coming home to the truth of your experiences. You stop waiting on the world to love your dark skin, to crown you *Nigra Sum Et Formosa*.[17] (They're about five hundred years behind—you'd be waiting forever.)

You stop abandoning the dark-skinned girls you were before and how they show up today for some false sense of unity, some "greater good" of conflict avoidance.

You, your honest feelings, and all the dark-skinned girls you were before *are* the greater good.

And not to get all spoken-word-poetry on you, but darkness is gorgeous. I love the contrast of the whites of your eyes to the drowning-black-brown of your irises, adore the way your skin specifically reminds me of the home that exists in the memory of my cells, love seeing how your skin kisses the edges of magenta, bright white, turquoise. I love seeing your dark skin set against bubble baths and blue lights.

Whether the dark-skinned girls you were before are in denial, victimhood, indignation, self-blame, or a muddy, overlapping mixture of each stage, know that this is all forgiveness. You are *always* on the path

---

17 *"Nigra sum et formosa*/I am black and beautiful" is a Bible verse from Song of Solomon 1:4–5. The verse was once inscribed on the Madonna of Montserrat, one of the many famed "Black" Marian figures of Europe. Here I replace the "sed" (meaning "yet") with a more truth-baring "et" (meaning "and"), just like my mother's favorite 1990s hair relaxer, Dark & Lovely, a darkness that amplifies beauty.

towards an integrated survival, however indirect.

Feel it *all*, for every emotion always leads back to love.

I and the Dark-Skinned Girls I was before walk together now, louder than sad, laughing even, because only some of us are brave enough to glow in the dark.

HONEYKNIFE PRAXIS

- **Drip:** Name your skin color as if it's a new Crayola shade—except for Midnight Coffee because that's one of mine (this exercise was introduced to me by yoga revolutionary Felicia Savage Friedman). Repeat whenever you desire.
- **Drizzle:** Write a letter to your junior high self. Soothe her wounds and worries.
- **Pour:** Find the best colors for your skin, the ones that make your skin color pop. Wear them often.

4

Crybaby

I reached my zenith of tears in fifth grade. Mariah Carey's "Always Be My Baby" was my favorite song. The summer before school started, my parents threw me a gigantic party complete with three outfit changes, a bounce house that deflated mid-party due to a short-term power outage in the city (I will never forget the uncle yanking screaming children from inside like a Heineken tipsy firefighter), and a Little Mermaid cake with teal buttercream frosting.

Only one person to whom I extended handwritten invitations showed up, a typical feature of being friends with white/Brown girls who didn't really like you and/or had parents who thought you lived on a block full of drive-bys and easily accessible cocaine. But Nerissa Galvan had her parents drop her off. She had a Dora the Explorer bob and wide hazel eyes. I escorted her around the party as if I were a translator bridging her experience into my Nigerian American universe, pointing out the jollof rice and the tub of iced malts.

My favorite dress was a blue sequin puff skirt A-line number with matching shoes dyed and bedazzled with craft store rhinestones. There is a picture of me, incandescent and laughing, dancing with my dad as aunties and uncles spray me with dollar bills.

By the next year, I was the resident crybaby of Homeroom 18. Perhaps puberty's imminent arrival was already spooking my hormones into a whirlwind of emotional dysregulation. Or maybe some deep, dark, and ancient ghost was early-bird mourning the demise of my girlhood. In fifth grade, I was eye-level with my homeroom teacher and slightly taller than my

57

mother, an exposed nerve with the dimensions of a junior policewoman.

My tears had no chill. I cried for everything.

- Being picked last for a school game of Whacko! (baseball but replace baseball bat and ball with tennis ball and racket).
- When I lost the fifth grade spelling bee because I misheard the word, ending my two-year first place reign ('til this day, I deeply detest the word "redecorated").
- When I ran for school secretary and lost to Shawna Arroyo, bitter defeat seeping from my eyes as I walked home alone.
- When my mother's voice moved too close to ice or when my father's temper leaped too near to fire.
- When a geologist presented at a school assembly and there was a raffle for a geode of amethyst. I didn't win and so I cried.
- I even cried during a fight with a teacher's blonde son after a game of keep away went awry because he called me a bitch. I also hit him and got suspended.

If my crying was a crested graph with x and y plotlines, the summit would register fifth grade as record tearfall. For years, when I remembered these scenes from my life, an involuntary cringe would quake from forehead to neck. If there were a movie of my life that I once hoped would go straight to DVD, never to be seen by large or attentive audiences, this period would be my crybaby years. Better still, I'd abandon these crying scenes on the cutting room floor and lock them into a basement labelled Excess, taking them out only when I was ready to douse them with lighter fluid and burn them into nothing.

Because the truth is also this: I was a hurting girl with a cavernous desire to be seen. I often felt invisible and unimportant. When I cried, people paid attention to me. Sure, their reactions were a mixed bag of exasperated teachers and doting team dads, but sometimes my heart was a goblin for attention. How I wished to be that storied, stoic Black girlchild I was always reading about in Scholastic books. I hated how my tears told on me, how they erupted even when I tried my best to clench them back in a cinematic revolt of puckered brows, wet cheeks, helpless rolling girl shoulders, and easily hurt soul, but I also loved being seen too.

I remember in my late twenties, watching *12 Years a Slave* in an arthouse theater and knowing that if my ancestors had faced the brutality of the trans-Atlantic slave trade, my countenance would probably not be that of the enduring Harriet Tubman. I could pretend, but my tears would tell on me. My sensitivity moved me closer to Eliza, who in the film and book is a freed Black woman who was forced into slavery. In the book and film, Eliza's sexual "relationship" with her master drew the ire of her mistress, and she was sold, only to be subsequently separated from her own two children. A rag is stuffed inside Eliza's mouth to stifle her crying, and Solomon Northrup, the protagonist of the film, is instructed to play his violin to mute her tears as she is sold away.

By nature and nurture, sensitive Black girls feel the edges of life acutely and this makes us especially vulnerable to playground hierarchies and disdain. Some of us swallow down the hurt or channel our vulnerability into armor where we become the bully. Some of us become crybabies.

My tears embarrassed people, annoyed them. Years past my fifth-grade bout of crying, a friend tells me that whenever I would cry and receive a hug from my teacher, she would roll her eyes behind my back. My mom tried to wean my emotional displays away. She'd tell me about the sticks and stones and breaking bones and that I didn't have to cry.

And slowly, I became the girl who didn't.

I learned to bury my tears into a place on the right side of my abdomen and to heap on the self-deprecating humor. I became an expert at closing my throat so the feelings would never reach my eyes.

But then, sometimes I was not so lucky. A hard word, a basketball game gone bad, a slap would puncture my careful, passive façade.

The dam would break.

And my crybaby would return triumphant.

I know how strong you are.

I know how much you've had to keep it together, stuff the disappointment and hurt so far behind your liver that it transfigured into rage. I know how many people walked past your tears, pretend-comforted you, and then rolled their eyes behind your back because Black girls are only supposed to cry when a bullet enters the scene.

Do you remember that one part in *Queen & Slim*?

I saw the movie on opening day at Regal Cinemas, in the La Habra movie theater my family has visited for over twenty years. There were six people in the theater: me, my sister, two white girls, and a couple. He was Black, she was Latina.

I thought the movie was going to be about two very cute dark-skinned people falling in love against a Bonnie and Clyde style soundtrack. I was surprised when the couple fought most of the one-hundred and thirty-two minutes and at how much physical pain Queen is in for most of the film. She is the first one shot, the first to die. It dismays me how marketable Black female pain is.

Racism is a nightmare, but it's strange how casually people share police brutality videos as if they are adorable cat outtakes. A millennial scholar with way more gore tolerance and a PhD might attempt to school me on the merits and need for Black horror, to which I agree: Black artists should explore whatever they want. We too deserve to express the full spectrum of our humanity, and this includes blood, death, murder. I as the viewer hold the responsibility of knowing which art is for me. Currently, I am stuffed full of the buffet of violences to Black bodies. I rarely need another serving.

In one scene, Queen escapes from a two-story window and her shoulder is painfully dislocated. Slim needs to push the shoulder back into place. He gives Queen a piece of fabric to bite down on.

"I think there are cops out front, and if they hear you—it's over. We're done. I know how strong you are," Slim says.

Queen nods—and then with a quickness, he pushes her bone back in. With her scream strangled by his shirt, they are now free to run to their

60

death. I know her sound would have killed them—but I wanted to hear her pain, wanted it to explode off the screen like Merry Clayton's howl in the Rolling Stone's "Gimme Shelter." I wanted to hear how much she hurt.

There should be a members-only slideshow that every Black girl is invited to on her sweet sixteen, rotating images of crying Black women unleashing a variety of tears: for wedding heartbreak, professional disappointment, birth of child, skinned knee, bruised ego, orgasmic ecstasy. An old Black woman with silver locs past her knees would crown each girl with a halo of marigolds, granting her permission to feel the fullness of her life's every tear.

And maybe she would tell her in every Black girl language she knew: it's okay to cry.

I wanted Queen to cry like that. Wailing, snot-nose, eyes squeezed shut into slits-cry.

I know I am asking the impractical.

In the end scene, Queen and Slim being murdered by police officers is a brutally beautiful ballet of slow motion, wide frames, and an explosion of red. For a few breathy moments, I almost believed they might just escape to Cuba. After the movie, me, my sister, and the couple remained in our seats, almost immobile, long past the credits.

The two white girls left giggling, throwing popcorn into their mouths.

I love the Strong Black Woman.

Half-fake and yet real, she is the costume we are instructed to slip on when life and people are cruel. There was always something about my mom's anger (when it wasn't directed at me) that I adored. It's the Aries in me. I loved how bravely she showed up for herself. I loved how big she would get when treated unfairly by the Petty Racist Association of North Orange County suburbanites in the aisles of Ross, TJ Maxx, Smart & Final. While there was a part of me that wanted to fold myself in between the crack of floor tiles because I hated displaying emotional volatility with white witnesses, there was another part of me that was positively ecstatic to be aligned with her warrior feminine energy, her blatant display of autonomy and self-respect.

The Strong Black Woman is who raised me. The Strong Black Woman is who I want to be and who I am, even if She arrives more quietly than my foremothers.

And yet.

Hypertension and high blood pressure are real things. Being the Strong Black Woman is work. I am disturbed with the mythology that surrounds the Strong Black Woman and the expectations that Black women are inherently hard, abrasive, and invulnerable.

Black Macho and the Myth of the Black Superwoman was written by Michelle Wallace, a feminist, critic, and the daughter of artist Faith Ringgold, in 1979 when she was only twenty-seven years old. She was promptly vilified and ostracized for her offering. Wallace was one of the first scholars to specifically tackle what we now call *misogynoir*, a term describing intra-racial sexism and anti-Black racism first coined by queer Black feminist Moya Bailey. The bravery of those second- and third-wave Black feminists is the reason I write with anything like freedom; my outlook is their legacy. They are how I learned that it was possible to be both strong and sensitive.

I have very little romantic appreciation for the Struggle that made the Strong Black Woman so strong, the legacies of violence, the stupefying neglect. Those legacies can go kick rocks and kick them hard. In fact, whenever I think of this mythological Black woman strength, I see a certain scene in *Napoleon Dynamite*, the 2004 cult sleeper hit that I watched on repeat my first year in military school crowded around laptops with my friends. In the movie, Napoleon's dorky older brother Kip is selling some Tupperware-like material around their small Idaho town. The job is not one he wants in the least. To demonstrate the tenacity of the plastic for a potential customer, Kip decides to run it over in his van, boasting of its invincibility. The Tupperware cracks instantaneously. Kip drives away in whiny disappointment.

That plastic bowl is Black woman strength.

The van is the world.

Black women live amongst people who praise our resilience, treat our souls as crash-test dummies for abuse.

It may be awhile yet before many unlearn this tendency.

Instead of waiting for their evolution, I hope you will remember this: it is okay to cry.

You might've grown up in households with all kinds of unmetabolized hurt going on, and your emotional vulnerability was seen as a threat to the careful balance of survival. This dissonance extends beyond the home into the general culture. The standard of white womanhood commemorates physical and emotional weakness; it award damsels in distress who overly rely on masculine strength to fill in the gaps.

In paradoxical fashion, for Black girls and women, strength becomes a weakness. Unfortunately for us, people can be kind of stupid about strength. They do not always care softly for the strong—they beat them against rocks and handle them roughly until they prove their durability, forgetting that even the strong can receive tenderness.

But you don't need additional theory on what the Black Woman as Superwoman does to your soul. You know the heaviness. You know how this repression of our disappointment, hurt, and despair arrives in dulled eyes, tight smiles, simmering anger, and stress-related diseases that steal years of life. It is okay to acknowledge the weight of those expectations and the impossibility of fulfilling them, along with the limited ways you have approached your hurt in the past.

It is okay to cry.

I really wish I had one of those elegant crying woman faces—one lone tear rolling down my cheek, *Casablanca* style. Instead, I resemble a toddler post-tantrum—wavy mouth and puckered eyes. This is why I hate crying in public. Today, vulnerability and authenticity are the new self-esteem, an almost-requirement for public-facing capitalistic success. Vulnerability is defined as "capable of being physically or emotionally wounded" or "open to attack or blame" (Merriam-Webster). Vulnerability is a revelation of our not-so-shiny parts, an honesty about what we carry as our shame. Vulnerability is a practice of forgoing our protective covers and masks and standing naked in our humanity.

And vulnerability can be a bit of a bitch.

When Black women are more rewarded for our mask than our emotional reality, when we are already so deeply misunderstood, is it cowardly or is it smart to be mindful of who we share our shame with? When women who are not Black tell me to speak affirmations attesting to how the world is "a safe space to be all of you," it feels as if they are guides cloaked in invisibility and bulletproof skin urging me to run naked into a field lined on both sides with emotional landmines.

"Tell us how you really feel," they say.

"Be open. Be honest. Be you," they say.

I have read countless self-help books promising that emotional trans parency will free us all. I understand how deeply crucial it is for humans to fully express their emotional selves, so I want to believe them, I really do. But I keep thinking of Sandra Bland[18] and her honest anger. After a police officer stopped her without due cause, she expressed her anger and her

---

18 Sandra Annette Bland was found dead in her cell, three days after being stopped for a traffic violation in 2015. Her death was ruled a suicide, but there are many realities that complicate this narrative. It is no secret that Black women face a double whammy when it comes to American social discourse. We are too often ignored by domestic violence statistics and made invisible during police brutality protests. Even though Black women are the group of women most likely to be murdered by police, making up one third of all police brutality deaths, it took the #SayHerName social movement to bring these deaths to the forefront. In 2020, 1,821 Black women were murdered in the United States. That's 5 Black women every single day. The obvious fact is that most of the time when a woman is murdered, cis or trans, the perpetrator is a male domestic partner. We do not like to talk about these perpetrators because it would mean being honest about the realities of sex work in a misogynistic and violence-based society, the casual emotional and physical terrorism Black women face in our communities, and the intricacies of speaking about violence when there are no direct white people to blame. There has not been a ton of attention to Black femicide, even though Black women die by homicide at a rate more than twice that of white women. My hope is that we stop normalizing these deaths, that police officers who misuse their power are held accountable, and that we find and create our own oasis of safety because this current world order is just not it.

fear. And now, she is no longer alive on this earth.

Despair was not an expression that my foremothers had the luxury of displaying. We are Black daughters who were applauded when we got angry but not when we were just plain broken by grief. We are dark-skinned girls whose skin is loaded with fables about our invulnerability. And because we respect our ancestors and their fortitude, crying feels close to betrayal.

You are not strong because of how many vans have ridden over your worth, not expecting you to break. You are strong because though you have been hurt, you still choose to love and allow yourself to be loved.

Your love is your superpower.

Black woman strength is less about durability and more about a spectacular courage. Sometimes, the bravest thing we can do is cry: to let hot tears snake down our cheeks and wet our shirt; to make ugly sounds straight from the heart's gut; to watch as our tears mix in with the shower's splash, carried down the drain; to face whether we are using our tears as manipulation and accountability avoidance.

We may not live in a world that can hold our tears.

There are so many police outside.

Still, there is an initiation afoot.

There's a chance for sensitive Black girls and women to transform the police inside our own souls, the forces inside that judge us when we voice our pain. These hypercritical reprimands are phantoms of shame. We can stop continuing their efforts to censor our pain.

We can allow our tears to just be.

If there were a crying award, I would be runner-up:

I cried in a Toronto bathhouse.

And on public bus B79.

I cried on basketball benchwarmer sidelines.

And in front of a Dunkin Donuts employee before ordering a glazed coconut.

I cried at an art museum magic show.

And in a Regal Cinemas bathroom stall after watching *A Star is Born*.

I cried sitting in the dim of a burlesque theater.

And curled up in the corner of a three-star Las Vegas hotel.

I cried walking past a graveyard after a '90s dance party.

And in a crusty bar decorated with overlapping punk stickers.

We often wait for big moments—that break-up, that death—for permission to cry, but your tears deserve release whenever they desire.

Whenever you can, wherever you feel safe to do so: cry. I am not saying you must go all Mary Magdalene and film yourself crying on TikTok. I am only saying that you do have something to cry about.

And that it is okay to cry.

One of my favorite films is *Children of Men*, based on the book by P.D. James and directed by Alfonso Cuarón. In the film, a dystopian future is marked by misery, immigrant blame (mostly immigrants of color nicknamed "fugees"), climate and economic crisis, and widespread infertility. Not a fun world. It's discovered that a Black woman refugee named Kee is carrying the world's first baby in eighteen years, a miracle child that the entire world wishes to claim and keep. With the protection of the antihero, Theo, a pregnant Kee embarks on a journey to escape the political forces who wish to steal her child and claim it as their own. Their fates intertwined, Kee flees with Theo towards their only hope—a humanitarian vessel called *Tomorrow*.

Kee and Theo make their final stop at a dismal refugee camp, where Kee delivers her baby in the cold of night. The next day, a full-scale refugee riot erupts. The hot fire of guns and bombs rips through the camp. Lifeless, bloodied bodies litter the ground. Smoke rises from the destruction.

As Kee and Theo move towards their final escape, the war outside suddenly quiets.

The camp is blanketed in an awesome silence.

For, the cries of a baby Black girl are heard.

After eighteen years of worldwide infertility, the newborn's presence is life itself.

A long, uninterrupted panning shot follows Kee and Theo and the baby as they descend the stairs of a bombed out building. Soldiers, old women, and freedom fighters peer at the child in hopeful wonder. With her cries, every person recognizes that the world is truly born again. This baby Black girl with the name of Dylan moves the world towards tomorrow.

Slowly but surely, with a shit ton of therapy and the trust of those who loved me, I learned to cry without shame. Of course, my old conditioning shows up: the white teacher rolling her eyes, my mother or father telling me that crying was a choice I could avoid. This energy may never leave me completely. But I know without a doubt, in moments more plentiful than not, that my tears, my hurt, my sadness are just as welcome as my rage and my happiness.

Trust the crybaby of your soul.

Let those tears have their red carpet debut with the ones who can hold them.

May you find those who can hold your pain as much as your strength.

May one of those people be you.

May you cry for all those who came before you who could not.

May you cry for all those who come after you so that they know they are allowed to feel every seed of their sorrow, that they are worth this pleasure too.

Your tears contain the diamonds of your genius.

Your tears are a relief and a release.

Your tears are a mighty container.

But, if you hear anything, anything at all, just know this—

It is okay to cry.

HONEYKNIFE PRAXIS

- **Drip:** Write a letter from and to your sad little girl self. Allow her to express her disappointment and hurt with full abandon. Respond to her as you wish a caring someone had done for you.
- **Drizzle:** Let yourself cry. Let the tears fall. Dare yourself not to apologize.
- **Pour:** Complete a session of trauma-aware breathwork with a professional, online or in person. Continue if you feel called to this work.

5

COMPASSION!®
An Empathy-Life Game®

When I was spit out from the mouth of the US Merchant Marine Academy onto the shores of my first duty station in Portland, Oregon, I entered what Dr. Valorie Thomas calls a "diasporic vertigo." Thomas coined the phrase as a "motif of decolonization" to describe the feeling that Black bodies encountered once they entered the New World as enslaved workers, stripped from their homes and sense of self. This vertigo is still on repeat across generation. Diasporic vertigo is a space that moves between chronic disconnection and healing resistance simultaneously, a constant toggling between being wounded, being the wounder, and being the healer all in the same moment. The ground is always moving; the answers hardly simple.

I was in my early twenties in mid-aughts Portland, awkward and searching in my keffiyeh scarf and braided sideswept bangs. My life felt like a yin and yang tattoo, a dualistic monism of conservative values and radical politics. I was being paid regularly and well by the United States of America for inspecting commercial vessels and standing command duty officer watch. I wore a blue operational uniform and saluted the flag. People thanked me for my service; I said "you're welcome" and meant it.

In my heart of hearts, I was a wannabe punk. Too fond of middle class niceties like parental approval, tulip festivals, and pineapple mimosas to do any real anarchist damage, I spent a lot of my time loitering around the edges of radical movements. I stood in the front row at a festival for Black punks as light-skinned alt kids yelled earnestly about masturbation and capitalism. I visited the Occupy tents in downtown Portland, read the *Shotgun Seamstress*,[19] and made zines about Yoruba goddesses.

Merriam-Webster defines compassion as "sympathetic consciousness of others' distress together with a desire to alleviate it." Compassion is a diasporic vertigo between self and other—how much we care whether we're hurting people and how much we are willing to do something about it.

I have long been a student of compassion from teachers as diverse as bell hooks to Jesus Christ. There are days I feel like a New Age Care Bear, stomach shining forth with Martin Luther King rainbows and Mother Teresa glitter. But sometimes people suck. Violence erupts all around us, and then I'm hearing Stokely Carmichael's infamous quote, "In order for nonviolence to work, your opponent must have a conscience. The United States has none." I longed for easy answers, a political movement, a manifesto that made compassion simple.

In my mid-twenties, I was a certified intergroup facilitator. This mainly meant co-leading dialogues on race and racism for an assortment of city employees, equity and inclusion specialists, and racially clueless soft-hearted hippies.

We met in a city office building decorated with social justice factoids and flat corporate carpeting. There was the diversity mandated cheese pizza and flat coke. We were getting through Week three or four, well past the "common definitions" exercises on posterboard where we all agreed that racism isn't just *not being nice to people* but a form of systemic racial prejudice and abuses of power. Week four was usually where conversations melted into wilder, more fertile territory, well past *I don't care if*

19 A serial zine and ode to Black punk culture lovingly and meticulously created by Nigeri-an-American musician, zinester, and ceramist Osa Atoe. The zine featured seminal Black punk and alt figures such as Vaginal Davis, Poly Styrene, and Brontez Purnell. The zines were published in book form by Coffee House Press in 2022.

you're green, blue, or purple. Discussion and debate finally breaks open to dialogue.

Unfortunately, one night, the conversation stalled.

There was a white woman, Baby Boomer status, curly brown hair—and she was crying. White women tears currently disrupt the space/time continuum, so there I was, watching as weeks of careful building collapsed with Jenga tumult. I do not recall exactly what produced her tears, but I do recall mention of a Black nanny. I also remember, pristine like the edges of a snowflake, that my heart, usually warm with empathetic overidentification with the distress of others, felt like Novocain mouth.

I consider empathy to be a strength and feeling this stretch of nothing was frightening. I was so used to feeling too much.

The journal of Lauren Oya Olamina, the protagonist of Octavia Butler's science fiction Parable series, starts July 20, 2024. In the series, which details a post-dystopian California full of cute things like environmental collapse, cultural wars, and corporate greed, Lauren has a condition called "hyperempathy," a self-fulfilling delusion that she can feel others' pain just as much as her own. Her extremely sensitive system causes her to feel the landmines her community refuses to acknowledge, though she cannot easily fall into violence because if she punches someone in the face, *she* will feel the crushed jawbone. Lauren inherited this condition from her mother, who was addicted to a prescription drug called Paraceto while Lauren was in utero.

Off the page, Octavia Butler's life was no stranger to cruelty. Bookish, shy, extremely tall, and growing up in white suburbia in 1950s Pasadena, she was taunted by schoolmates and describes a pretty lonely girlhood. It is difficult to ingest meanness and not spit it right back where it came from, a quandary that Butler wrestled with in much of her work. Sometimes humans behave more like prey and predator than like a cooperative species that needs each other to survive. And who knows this fact more intimately than a Black woman like Butler? She was often the only Black face in the world of science fiction; she took the public bus in a West Coast area she dubbed "Jim Crow California."

Compassion is a layered experience, with more grey than stark black and white. What has helped me move towards a more balanced compassion is to treat compassion like a game.

The incentive?

Keeping your soul.

The players?

Fortunately and unfortunately, everyone and everything on earth.

The first order of COMPASSION!® is boundaries—the limitations between other and self.

I slapped a man once. I hadn't been in a physical fight since fifth grade when a blonde boy called me a *bitch* and landed me a suspension. When I slapped a man on the Lower East Side, I was in my late-twenties, exiting a summer burlesque show with a new friend. In true New York City fashion, a man in a nice dress shirt decided it would be fun to sexually harass my friend. My friend politely demurred and I stayed silent, hoping he would take the hint and leave.

He did not take the hint.

One block became two. Two became four. Finally, I faced him, wondering if maybe he was on something: "Look, dude, she doesn't want to talk to you."

The man's face grew mean like a baby suddenly separated from a pacifier. I had half expected this. Some men do not react well to feminine boundaries, especially when these boundaries come from a woman with visible muscle.

He said, "What are you, some type of man?"

This was not the first time I had been publicly shamed or harassed for not being the right kind of woman according to a very loud-mouthed stranger.

"Sure, I'm a fucking man," I said, and then I slapped him.

Not slap-your-mother-into-next-week slap, but a hearty wake-up to the cheek, nonetheless.

He and I argued stupidly for a bit amongst the drunk groups of club goers and the Ubers weaving their way down the avenue. He wanted to brawl but was unsure what gender rules applied. I shouted threats that I had no desire to fulfill. Eventually, he was pulled away by his friends, and my friend and I left, descending the paint-scuffed steps of the subway.

"I can't believe you slapped that dude," she said once the two of us sat down on a halfway-full A train. There was a caution in her voice, maybe because she believed that I walked the streets of Manhattan picking fights with weird men.

"Me either," I replied.

We never hung out again.

What I did was wrong, and yet, even now, I do not feel absolute regret. Before this incident, I *have* walked away when others said horrible things about my body, saying nothing. I have taken the path of least resistance, so frozen inside by shame and overwhelm that I could barely access the power to speak. That night, I was not just slapping that man—and that was the problem. I was slapping every man before him who had used his power to harm and expected that I would not fight back. For years, I did not. That day, my self-compassion (and my anger) loomed larger than my fear, and I did. I used my words. And then I used my hands.

Butler never quite answers whether Lauren Olamina's compassion overdrive is a superpower or a super detriment in *Parable of the Sower*. Lauren can be weakened by another's injury, but her condition also makes it less likely she will hurt others (even those who deserve retaliation). In several interviews, Butler was adamant that Lauren's condition is a delusion.

In Butler's work, Lauren is the founder of "Earthseed," a spirituality whose central ethos is that "God is Change." This spirituality was largely inspired by the Yoruba goddess figure Ọya. Ọya, often pictured as a beautiful, tall, and dark-skinned warrior-woman wearing a skirt of nine colors, represents the great winds of life and shakes up the roots of stagnation. Lauren made many moral choices that are not easily coded as right or wrong in her quest to evolve beyond violence.

Here we are, dear Earthling, tenderly transforming our relationship to COMPASSION!® The game of COMPASSION!® is a voice situated between savagery and doormat. This voice is you and not you: quiet, still, and firm.

Some call this voice the Goddess Within, others the Conscience, some others Wisdom. I call her Compassion. She is not aggressive; she is honest about when you are in the wrong. She is not passive; she is real about when you are being taken advantage of. She is not swayed by your excuses and the wail of your inner critic.

You will know this voice because she is helpful. She does not just insult your past or fearmonger about the future; she offers a way, a pause that allows your inborn reaction to graduate into a compassionate response, one that honors the self and the other with room to grow.

During the winter of 2018, I attended a weekend meditation retreat specifically designed for Black people and people of color outside of Baltimore. The air was crisp. I sat cross-legged amongst activists, organizers, and people who desired an ancestral inheritance beyond survival, who were willing to practice a new compassion. While I knew my journey on this field called compassion was hardly over, there were some closures. I no longer held resentment at the crying white woman or the man who misgendered me; I accepted that their evolution was none of my concern and that they had helped me move into more complex understandings of compassion. I no longer needed an easy right or wrong. But, I still had some questions, and so I asked the meditation teacher, a Black woman and a former Buddhist nun, "How does one hold compassion for those people who are unwilling or unable to extend the same grace to you?"

The meditation teacher smiled in an almost supernatural calmness that spoke of her years of study alongside Thich Nhat Han. If there was going to be anyone who understood the game of COMPASSION!® and how to find solid ground between the part of us that is wounded and the part of us that still desired to extend grace and heal, or at the very least, not hate another human being, it was her. She listened to me and there was still an easy smile when she shared her answer. It was an answer that gave me access to a new understanding of compassion that did not ignore the vertigo. Her answer provided a grounding that allowed me to access my deepest compassion within.

She did not tell me to play nice in Buddhist speak.

She did not say that my question was wrong.

She said, "When you cannot offer compassion for others, then offer compassion for the part of you that desires to but cannot."

HONEYKNIFE PRAXIS

- **Drip:** Perform a random act of compassion for a stranger, friend, relative, or even yourself. How does it feel to alleviate someone's suffering?
- **Drizzle:** Sit and meditate on lovingkindness—first for someone you really love, then for someone you feel neutral about, and then for an enemy. How does it feel to wish well on these different types of people?
- **Pour:** Live a life of compassion. Do unto others as you would have done unto you. Pretend that compassion is the new punk.

Interlude 2

Interlude 2:
From Struggle to Peace

Olódùmarè, the Supreme Creator Being in Yoruba spirituality, sent seventeen orisa down to earth to get the world right. Save for Òsun, all the orisa were male. These orisa included Ogun (god of iron and workmanship), Ṣàngó (god of lightning and thunder), and Orunmila (god of wisdom and destiny). These orisa didn't think they needed Òsun's help with creation. It was like the worst example of a high school group project.

Never *once* were they like, "Hey Òsun, we need a hand here." Òsun was rightfully pissed off (and pregnant), and yet the male orisa continued their worldbuilding totally unbothered. These orisa worked and worked, but the world was without flow. Chaos, destruction, and despair ruled the land. Finally, the sixteen male orisa fled back to Olódùmarè full of complaint and confusion.

"Why was everything so shitty?" they whined.

Olódùmarè, sighed in Supreme Being fashion, "I sent seventeen of you to earth but only sixteen stand before me," and then They[20] said, "What about Òsun?"

---

20 Though many scholarly and spiritual retellings, scholars, spiritualists, and diviners assign "He" and "Him" descriptions to Olódùmarè, there is no specific gender for this being. Alternatively called Olorun and Oluwa, Olódùmarè is the supreme ruler of the universe in Yoruba spirituality, the omnipotent source of all that is—good, bad, indifferent. Part of the obsession on naming God as He/Him is no doubt because of the pesky fly that is patriarchy. When God = Man, male leadership seems "natural," predetermined, and limited to aspects that traditionally govern and safeguard masculine behavior. (contd.)

Òsun, Chief Mother and the One Who Dances.[21]
Òsun, Righteous Seductress Who Is Also Vulture.
Òsun, Mother of the Mirror.

"Did you guys really think you could build a world without her?"

And so the orisa ran back to Òsun with throats full of *sorry* and *my bad*, but Òsun was not having it. She decided to make a deal with them. If the child she carried was a daughter, she was *so over it*. But, if the child she carried was a son, she would lend her hand and help the orisa rebuild their world into a paradise, a real heaven on earth.

Thankfully, for these orisa, Òsun gave birth to a bouncing bundle of XY. Looking into her son's bottomless black eyes, she knew she could not leave the earth hanging on by a thread—even though she was tired of being overlooked and wanted to tell these orisa to go screw themselves. She smiled at the orisa, knowing that her power was so great that it only took one of her for every sixteen of them. And with that pride, she helped create a new world.

Where there is struggle, there is peace.

Peace is: ease, softness, contentment, and the absence of difficulty or worry. Every location of struggle in our lives is an opportunity to discover the calm at the center of the storm and become this center. Òsun was chosen as afterthought to build the world, and that world failed spectacularly until she took charge.

You only need a drop of honey. It only took one Òsun to right the world

---

Naming spiritual power as feminine and autonomous cracks open the farce of patriarchy, revealing the incompleteness of its worldview. Another reason Olódùmarè tends to slip between gender expressions is the linguistic queerness of the Yoruba language itself. Yoruba hosts many unisex names, and while it does house specific gender categories of woman (obinrin) and man (ọkunrin), it does not carry specific gender pronouns like she/he or even daughter/son. Things therefore get a little fun in translation. I often use capital letter "They" whenever I reference Olódùmarè in a gesture towards being a little truer to the unlimited expression of this Being. Some writers and scholars use "She" for this Being to honor Her creative aspects. I dig that, too.

21 Italicized titles of Òsun are provided via Awo Fa'Lokun Faunmbi's *Oshun: Ifa and the Spirit of the River* (original publication, 1993).

into balance. Initially, she wanted to meet their exclusion with a grand exit, but she knew that a world without her healing would be a world that her son, her blood, could not live in. And so, ever the ethical goddess, she decided to take her place in the assembly of creation.

Never forget: your struggle is a portal to peace.

6

Lion Daddy

"Iya ni wura. Baba ni jiggi."
"Mother is gold. Father is mirror."
—Yoruba proverb

From the ages of thirteen to twenty-three, I played hundreds of games—organized basketball, specifically. Initially I was so unathletic upon taking the court for the first time in seventh grade that the head coach exiled me to the sidelines for two weeks so I was not a hazard to the other players. Eventually, I grew into a solid player that coaches could safely integrate into practice. While UConn and Tennessee never did come knocking on my door, I was team captain and leader of block shots. At the college level, I played all four years with the US Merchant Marine Academy team and cried into the sweaty collar of my jersey on our last game.

Basketball was mainly my dad's idea. Nigeria, like 95 percent of the world, worships at the altar of soccer, but my father fell in love with basketball when he first emigrated to the United States. This was the Black Man as King NBA of Kareem Abdul Jabbar, Michael Jordan, and still skinny Shaquille O'Neal. I remember many afternoons sitting down with my sister and brothers as we all watched a Lakers game with my father sitting behind us on the couch, remote in hand.

So, when the flyer for the National Junior Basketball league came home with me from school one day in junior high, I should have known what was coming down the pike. My father became zealous for me and my siblings to become basketball stars. We were tall Black kids who needed money for college, and there wasn't exactly a trust fund available. Like most immigrant parents, my father put a lot of pressure on us about our academics. Every year, my father would buy me and my sibs homework books from teacher surplus stores that we were to complete in addition to work assigned in class. On sporadic occasions, my dad would ask us if we completed *his* homework. God bless your life if your answer was no.

But over time, the pressure attached to our grades became firmly attached to our athletic journey. I played on varsity and a host of travel teams, earning some lukewarm scouting from California universities, an Ivy League team, and notice from some Division-II schools. I had fun playing and enjoyed the trips to San Diego and the pride of seeing what my body could accomplish with dedication and follow-through. But I would be lying if I said that I *lived* for the game or dreamed of a WNBA contract like some of the girls I played with. I distinctly recall a tournament where my major excitement was the end game buzzer because it meant I could return to the copy of *Pride and Prejudice* stowed away in my gym bag.

When the head coach of the US Merchant Marine Academy scouted me after a tournament in Chicago, I was dismayed. I wanted to drop acid at NYU and major in Contemporary Film Studies, become a stoner-intellectual and study psychology. But my father fell in love with the idea of my being a naval officer and the tuition-free benefits that military school provided.

My father is a Lion Dad, a Black father who values discipline, ambition, and clear-cut goals. Lion Dads are powerful figures, equally bite and roar, who believe in the promise of tough love. I used to joke that the strictness of the Merchant Marine Academy had absolutely nothing on my dad. At least in military school, the punishments were diffuse, mostly impersonal and consisted of pushups. Lion Dads are men denied opportunities from the outside world due to racism and colonialism and are hell-bent that their children conquer everything they were held back from. The burden of denied self-actualization typically falls on sons and daughters. We become the second chance, the living do-over, but of course this cycle deepens the pattern as we find ourselves denied the life we truly desired to live.

The Tiger Mom archetype was made famous in Amy Chua's 2011 memoir *Battle Hymn of the Tiger Mother* and brought the strict immigrant parent to the mainstream. Tiger Moms and Lions Dad are separated by geography, gender, and a host of other divisions, but I can really see them going out to brunch together based on their shared value systems alone. When survival and winning is the main goal, affection is an afterthought, if it is thought of at all.

I am a first-generation daughter who watched *The Breakfast Club* too many times. I wanted a Fun Dad, a cross between the purple anthropomorphic T-Rex Barney and Robin Williams before the divorce in *Mrs. Doubtfire*—one of those chill American fathers who engaged in pillow fights and late morning pancake art. This level of relaxation was never going to be the province of a man who had always worked, who believed that sleeping in was only for the infirm or the elderly. My dad dreamed of a neat professional daughter who wore pleated skirts and played in the WNBA. I failed to make the All-Navy basketball team not once but twice. I write books about ancient goddesses.

I grew up terrified of disappointing my father, scared of the way his irritation could volcano into rage, but I also wanted to make him proud. He emigrated to California in the late 1980s from a newly independent Nigeria with an degree in electrical engineering and was admitted to USC for a master's degree. But due to the glass ceiling afforded to Black men and the demands of raising a family of six in a new country unwelcoming to Black foreigners without deep pockets, he put his own aspirations on hold. Every day he woke up near dawn to go to work—at the convenience store we owned for half a decade; installing cables in Calabasas; learning JavaScript to code. For most of my life, work and my father were synonymous. I only interacted with him after his workday, when he was bone-tired and just wanted to be left in peace with his CNN.

Most of my friends and cousins had fathers who barely made cameo appearances in their lives, fathers who would call them out of the blue twenty-five years after abandoning them to ask for five hundred dollars or a place to stay. To them, our family, with a working father who sacrificed for his children every day, might as well have been the Nigerian version of the Cosbys. To share the complications of having a strict African dad only earned eye rolls and ire. And so, my rebellion went underground. My survival methods of choice were quiet obedience, an almost compulsive addiction to accomplishment, and a deep thirst for external recognition. I decided early on that if my father was going to see me, I wanted him to only see me as the best.

We all have daddy issues—long, patriarchal stories wrapping themselves around entire generations. We are everything our forefathers wanted, everything they detest. There are about 2.6 million single fathers for every 8.6 million single mothers, and about a third of children across race in America grow up without a father in their lives. Fatherlessness is a recurring topic with Black families across the diaspora. I know of far too many kids whose fathers largely disappeared from their lives, busy with pursuing their own pleasure.

I cannot divorce the realities of fatherlessness or complicated father bonds from racialized violence, from the limits of polygamist family structures, from the ways that men across generations have been socialized to overvalue their desires to the detriment of everyone else. Many Black fathers *are* deeply active in their children's lives, but their parenting is largely obscured by the prevailing narrative of the absent Black father. Animated Disney has a long tradition of matricide (see *Snow White*, *Cinderella*, *The Little Mermaid*, *Beauty and the Beast*, etc.) but when the time arrived to for an African-inspired storyline (*The Lion King*) or a Black-American tale of transformation (*The Frog Princess*), guess which parent went missing? (Disney offered a mea culpa in the 2020 animated fantasy film *Soul*, but the father exists primarily in flashback.)

Patriarchal (a word meaning "rule of the father") social systems are those with a clear hierarchy. They label anything that belongs to the realm of women, the female, and the femme as inferior and secondary. Some of us are born into families that resist this narrative and chill on the knee-jerk patriarchy antics. But the unearned power of patriarchy and the casualties that arise when we center domination as power are everywhere: violence, a severe lack of empathy, emotional immaturity, an allergic reaction to words like *accountability*. Patriarchal systems are feedback loops, generous in their repetition. Even our daddy issues have daddy issues.

I spent *years* throwing myself from one activist cause to the next, running from one spiritual promise to another, rarely connecting the dots between the anger I felt at my father's strictness and the righteous rage of political oppression. It was safer to deal with constitutional anger and disappointment than my own hurting heart.

Spiritual bypassing is defined as "the tendency to use spiritual ideas and practices to sidestep or avoid facing unresolved emotional issues, psychological wounds, and unfinished developmental tasks." The term was coined by John Welwood, a therapist and Buddhist teacher, in the mid-1980s. Examples of spiritual bypassing include trying to Wednesday Night Bible Study away your functional depression and deeply believing that a Seven Powers Candle will cure your avoidant-attachment style of romance.

Political bypassing is employing political ideas and practices to sidestep or avoid facing one's unresolved emotional issues, psychological wounds, and unfinished developmental tasks. This could look like signing every petition known to man, posting angry tirades on Facebook, or romanticizing The People when your own life is a dumpster fire of dismal self-care. It could mean enabling intra-group violence in the name of loyalty.

The first war many of us fight is how to survive as ourselves in our homes. Home is where I learned mutual care and play. It was also the place where I learned that life is not fair.

I was first recruited into the anti-racist army in seventh grade. My first reporting duty was a group called the Task Force, headed by my blonde English teacher and a man named Andre, who had the sexiest baritone I had ever heard. They were an Ebony and Ivory anti-racist couple who taught me early on what racism was beyond the personal. The Task Force met at the community center every month and talked about how to combat discrimination over Little Caesars pizza. We wore black T-shirts with a golden peace sign over the breast. We were adorable.

During the early aughts and in college, I was president of the Broadening Kings Point Association, where everyone with a melanin-count above 11 percent found refuge. While stationed in the Coast Guard in Portland, I trained as a facilitator for interracial intergroup dialogue sessions and was leader of our Human Relations Council. Aligning with anti-racism is and was healing, beautiful work. This work gifted me a sense of self-efficacy, compassion, and integrity. I have met some of the best humans in the world doing this work on every level. We were walking the path of those who came before us; we were creating a world that we wanted to live in.

But while anti-racism provided a safe space to discharge my rage, there were also limitations. Sometimes, my Blackness felt too firmly attached to racism, as if my relationship to white supremacy was the defining point of my skin. I'd find myself near addicted to analyzing the racial reality of any situation: *Was that barista rude to me because she was just annoyed at the macchiato foam or was it because of her proximity to colonization and implicit bias?*

Anti-racism, in its unevolved aspect, pigeonholes Blackness in the reactive, servile, and emotionally stunted role of a bruised child. We end up centering whiteness (again) in either reaction or attention, asking permission, and remaining watchful for the capricious attentions of this "daddy" to change. I sometimes wonder if anti-racism was clever indentured employment, strategic incompetence of the communal variety. I wonder about the current intellectual focus of anti-racism, whether it was creating intelligent-sounding bigots who knew how and when to quote James Baldwin but would never sit next to a Black man on a bus.

Toni Morrison wisely said that racism is a distraction because it takes you away from your work. You end up so focused on proving and teaching that you lose yourself. The roles I occupied to please the fathers of this land, including my own, distracted me for many years. I was always running, always angry, always wanting some outlet to divert me from what was really going on inside.

The perfect opportunity to stop this bypassing arrived when I left the Coast Guard in 2015. I spent five years in military school and six years on active duty. From the ages of eighteen to twenty-nine; I was always in a uniform. Military school, like my basketball career, was mainly a decision I made to be the kind of daughter my father would be proud of. But now I was free to choose what I wanted, and I wanted to know who I was beyond my anger, beyond the political bypassing I carried from my father's home out into the world.

One time, my sister sent me a video that made me cry. In 1976, Black middle-class families moved into a white working-class Queens, New York, suburb called Rosedale. Bill Moyers did a whole film about it. Save for pitchfork enthusiasm and disco handlebar mustaches, the scene is reminiscent of racialized gentrification divides occurring today. In the short documentary, a group of Black kids try to ride their bikes on a street only to be chased out and jeered at by enraged white children. The scene reads like some sensational orchestration, clearly uninterested in emotionally caretaking these Black children, because right after a very traumatic incident, the kids are immediately asked on camera how it feels to be hated so much.

The children range in age from about nine to fourteen, and they all exhibit markedly different, wholly appropriate responses to the racist incident. One girl in pigtails is visibly angry, face all scrunched up in pre-pubescent fury. Another kid solemnly promises to never forgive the white people. He is deflated and half shrugging: "They're never going to change." One girl cries silently, tears flooding her face. Another girl, long-faced and dark-skinned and probably the oldest of the group, speaks with big sister authority. "We're just human beings," she says. "I hate their guts," the pig-tailed girl says in reply. Long-faced girl shushes her gently, telling her not to say such a thing. Pig-tailed girl immediately starts crying into the arms of the oldest girl.

We survive abuse and hurt, personal or political, by adopting roles. We inhabit these cycles on repeat and then start to believe that this is *just who we are*. We learn, through threat of harm or harm itself, that it is safer to disown the entirety of who we are to please the daddy in our lives and that obedience is much safer than truth.

We may become obsessive achievers, constant fighters, or pleasing caretakers, or we may collapse into a defeated, escaping heap in our quest to be "loved" and accepted. The Rosedale children exhibited an intelligent, protective reaction to racialized trauma. No emotional reply was better nor more honest than the other. Whatever roles you have chosen to be safe in this world, know that they were the ones that helped you survive, and that is no small matter. We slip into these roles in both a personal *and* political sense, becoming a robotic repetition of whatever behaviors protected us from harm. To heal our father wounds and cease spiritual or political bypassing, whether they arose because our fathers were absent or present and unable to meet core needs, means bravely identifying our childhood roles, those costumes that once saved our lives but are now much too small for our adult selves.

The Mascot[22] role is where I reside most. This is the oldest child (and often the oldest generation), who is prized for their trophies and perfect attendance awards and has a predilection for too many degrees. Winning to us is when Black people are finally awarded a modicum of respect in the wider world: the athletes, the nationally recognized scholars and artists, the blue-ribbon firsts. Mascots are constantly in motion, barely pausing to register their amazing accolades. The family Mascot is afforded a seat at the table predicated on their ability to shine. The Mascot's success (usually against great odds) convinces the family that they are going to be okay. My

---

22 The roles I'm using here are augmented via John C. Friel's *Adult Children: The Secrets of Dysfunctional Families* (Health Communications, 1998).

Mascot role is the part of me living in the fantasy that to prove myself as valued and lovable, I have to achieve, win, repeat.

I was hustle personified, fleeing from frailties, and this has more than once resulted in me burning out. It turns out that holding unrealistic, perfectionistic ideals for self and others is not a great recipe for connection.

I am an Aries, born a day after my father's birthday. I love to win. And while excellence is beautiful, when my drive outweighs my ability to simply exist I am not really living. Nowadays, I check in with myself when I am thirsting for another recognition: Is this accomplishment for me or is it to prove my worth to someone (my dad, a used-to-be best friend, a naysaying teacher) or something (white people, feminine ideals, rich funders)?

Surprising to my inner critic, it is not a crime to be ordinary. I was not a stupendous basketball player or military officer, and the world did not implode into dust. Achievement is a hard addiction to shake completely, but I have drastically lessened my attachment to blue ribbons. I win for me first.

The Caretaker role cleans up the broken dishes and bandages wounds real and metaphorical. We're the supposed *bleeding hearts* running GoFundMes for our struggling friends and majoring in social work. When I am in caretaker mode, I feel most like myself when I am meeting the physical, mental, and emotional tolls that abuse exacts on others. My attention is tied to pleasing and serving while smiling; I tend to enmesh with the struggle of others.

The caretaker is seldom encouraged to help themselves or offered as much care as they give. This is the part of me living in the fantasy that I must keep the peace, care until I am numb, and please others above all else. Collectively, there is an expectation that Black people, Black women in particular, wipe the whitegirl tears, soothe the fragile egos, place themselves in service-oriented jobs (social workers, nurses, aides, teaching assistants) without equitable pay.

Caring is beautiful, but when I noticed that I was not extending the same care to myself, I knew it was time to pause. My mother and aunties are mainly nurses, from the LVN to RNs with master's degrees. I was taught that the highest call to goodness was to give. I believe this. But I also now know that caring for myself is a non-negotiable. I learned that many people will gladly take without thinking of the effect. I learned that those I extended care to could not magically read the buried resentment in my eyes—or did not want to.

I no longer pour from an empty cup. I meet the ego flex of martyrdom, releasing the idea that sacrifice is the pinnacle of love. I am more adept at asking for what I need, releasing the need to control others. A simple no is becoming one of my favorite words.

The Rebel role is all fight and outward action, respected and hated in equal measure. As a girl who sings in the tune of avoidant, I would not have been caught playing the part of heedless provocateur. But I could not deny the fight energy inside of me. The Rebel is a protective posture of agency. We meet life with fists up—even if we are punching the air.

Fighting back is beautiful, but chronic fighting was taking its toll in chronic body aches and battle-worn resignation. I have become better at choosing my battles and knowing which wars I am the most suited for. Black people are accustomed to fighting back against unjust power, but too often our humanity is squished into warrior without room for much else. By reminding myself of my dreams and taking action towards their fulfillment, I move beyond predictable reactions into personal power.

The Lost Child or Loner role inhabits entire worlds away from the family reality. This was the younger version of myself hiding in Narnia, making up elaborate daydreams and alternative universes, locked in my room or my head for hours upon hours alone. Lost children are sometimes easy to forget because when we hide, we hide so well.

Solitude is beautiful. In extroverted-favoring societies, we can become terrified of loneliness and hide away introspection. Lost or not, I am still of this earth and I can be myself where others can see. I belong to myself and the world simultaneously.

When we live wedded to the limitations of patriarchy or racism or abuse and these roles take up too much living space, we lose access to the totality of who we are and all we can be. Instead of moving through the world, heart open and free, we hide our tenderness. Instead of creating new paradigms for living, we spend precious energy explaining our existence to another human lost in the delusion of superiority. This to me will always be the saddest result of racism—how deeply this caste system rips us away from our true expression, forcing us to contort and perform for some semblance of safety. Violence creates a collective codependency where we lose sight of ourselves and our deeper desires. Over time, we *become* the compulsive habits and the reactions. Releasing these roles means we destroy the fantasy; we can never control another with our behavior, though it may be uncomfortable to release these illusions.

Growing up with a Lion Daddy means that I am ambitious, self-determined, and proud to be who I am. Knowing that racism is a noxious infestation helps me stay sane and centered in my own power. These are good things. What I am releasing day by day is the compulsive need to shrink myself into any one role for the benefit of a collective hierarchy that cares so little for my humanity. I have found that the best part of growing up is knowing that if you want to be free from old roles, you no longer have to wait on *any* daddy for permission. You can reparent your inner child so they evolve into a new paradigm where your reactive roles point to your strength. This is often slow, nonlinear, and devoted work, but the rewards (a sense of internal safety and kinder, honest relationships) speak for themselves.

You notice when your life feels wedded to the Mascot, Caretaker, Rebel, or Lost Child roles, inside and outside where you call home. You hold grace for why you held and hold onto these roles, what power they provided you, and what experiences created them. You find safe people who like you just as you are (you practice being that person first). You take gradual steps to divest from these roles and create a life more aligned with who you are and who you want to be.

This is no magic pill or sudden fix. Reparenting your inner child will take time, patience, and trial and error. Unfortunately for us, these systems and their legacies will not disappear overnight, no matter how much careful analysis and protesting we participate in. By meeting your reactive roles with compassion and by honoring your unmet needs and desires, you are an investor in an entirely new game: self-actualization for all.

About four months before COVID hit, I returned to the home of my childhood. I was burned out, mostly broke, and still nursing a broken heart from the end of my first committed romantic relationship. My family asked little and welcomed me back fully, allowing me space, time, and, let's not be coy, a rent-free life to write this book and get it together. There were no demeaning lectures, no hard asks.

During the initial summer months of lockdown, I visited a murky depression unlike anything I had ever experienced, thinking the sort of scary thoughts I had only read about in books. The only reason I emerged from this cave mostly unscathed from this dungeon was my family: my mother, my father, my sister, my brothers, and my friends who I see as blood.

The next summer, the world was barely out of the shadow of lockdown when I received a tryout email from Basketball Beauties, a vanity basketball league where mink eyelashes are queen. I missed basketball. The running, the sound of the ball against the court, the girl power of carefully executed offensive plays. Also, I had spent most of the pandemic going through intermittent yoga, Spotify dance breaks, and many, many tacos. Self-conscious about my COVID-15—the weight I had gained during lockdown—I signed up. I envisioned myself having one of those wild card basketball seasons where I became the surprise darling center of the league and showed off my stats to my dad.

In high school when I played basketball, there was no stomach churning event quite like running down the court, looking up, and seeing my father's intense stare in the stands. He was not able to make a lot of my games because of his busy work schedule, which I secretly loved. And so, when he did show up, my anxiety would shoot to level ten. I seemed to always make more mistakes during those games. He would catalog every run down the court, every missed layup, and more often than not, found my playing wanting. I remember too many tense car rides home, biting back tears, as he listed my every miss.

I also remember the first time my father told me he loved me. I was eighteen years old and leaving for my prep military school year at the New Mexico Military Institute. Tiger Moms and Lion Dads don't tend to favor effusive emotional expressions, and part of me was stunned when I heard those three words from him. There were tears in his eyes. I was so often searching for a love that I saw mirrored back by American TV dads, soft and cuddly, that I sometimes ignored the very real ways my father did show he loved me and my siblings—the way he was always there to escort me to shady mechanics, the Sam's Club grocery runs, his stint of finding me specialty dress shoes in high school because I was already a size 12 sophomore year. My father always showed up for us in the ways that he could, always chose to follow his ambition in ways I find remarkable in a country so rife with anti-Blackness and immigrant-fear. This is love too.

Like many Lion Daddies, my father has mellowed across age and experience. The early stresses of emigrating to a strange, cold country have melted and so has his roar. We watch *Jeopardy* together, and he even likes dogs now. He tells me to follow my dreams, which feels sort of surreal because when I was a teenager, my secret nickname for my parents was the Dream Killers. It's sometimes bizarre to reconcile this father, who sends me and my sister Neil deGrasse Tyson YouTube shorts and tells us to "just be happy," and finishes off most phone calls with "I love you," with the fiery patriarch, who would glance at my honor roll report card and still say it wasn't enough.

If I ignore the ways I was hurt in relationship to my father, I lie to the woman I am now and the girl I used to be. And if I do not acknowledge the ways he has grown, the ways he has supported my journey even when my journey was hella confusing and looked like a hot mess, and the ways he has had his own journey of reclamation and reparation, this is a void too.

I can carry both now, my anger and my hope, without having to escape into role playing or some other bypassing activity. I can stop playing games with my hurt. I can be with what is. Acceptance of our fathers, their strengths as well as their liabilities, is a form of love for ourselves where we tell our souls the truth. If you had a Lion Dad, there is probably a distance between what you needed and what you received. This is not your fault, nor is it a sin if you avoided this wound with a fog of bypassing and restrictive roles. We all do it.

In a patriarchal culture, there will also always be a distance between what your father needed and what he received. He is as much a product of the limitations of his era and boyhood as you are a co-creation of everything that raised you. This collective understanding of your father story does not mean condoning his abuse or abandonment. Your wounds and the spaces between your desires and reality are real, deserving of their own timeline of grief. While forgiveness is not mandatory for healing, understanding the forces that created your relationship with your father is.

Days before the Basketball Beauties season began, in true weekend-warrior-aging-athlete-mode, I reinjured my Achilles tendon during a pickup game with my brother at a small outside court in Brea. And yet, I stubbornly drove from Orange County to Chatsworth, a San Fernando Valley neighborhood located about four freeways away from me, to play basketball for six weeks.

It was arguably the worst basketball season of my life. Limping, in a bright yellow uniform about one and a half sizes too small, and surrounded by a swarm of light-skinned influencers, I gave it my all. At one evening practice, our coach felt so sorry for my gait that he basically begged me to sit out the final drills. When I hit the three-pointer that ended practice, I tried not to notice the screams of astonished delight from my very own teammates. In the shape I was in, I am sure they were impressed I was able to make any shot at all.

When I told my dad I was playing basketball again, probably while he was watching CNN in the living room, I'm sure he was not imagining his mid-thirties daughter, who was attending physical therapy for weakened ankles, was going to walk-on with the LA Sparks. "That's good," he may have said, patting me on the shoulder, mainly relieved that I was no longer amid a nervous breakdown. I probably could've said I had taken up trapeze fire breathing and he would have been happy and that's actually what felt good. To realize what had changed and what still remained. To know that we were father and daughter playing a new game.

HONEYKNIFE PRAXIS

- **Drizzle:** Breathe into where you are right now and know you are enough.
- **Drip:** What is one activity you wish you had shared with your father? Camping? Water color portraits? Conversations about your dreams? Find a good dude-esque person who is willing and able to explore this with you.
- **Pour:** Work with a trained mental health professional or spiritual guide to unearth your father wound and plant new seeds of self-love and trust.

7

Articulations of an Afro-Romantic

I inherited my romantic tendencies from my mom. She spent much of her girlhood in Ibadan voraciously reading Barbara Cartland novels and watching the bright, dazzling expertly choreographed romances of Bollywood. I poured over the age-inappropriate romance novels that my mother abandoned in our guest bedroom—slow burners by Danielle Steele and Judith Krantz that featured a flurry of hot queer sex scenes and may have inspired my softcore pillow goddess tastes. I loved that romance can be tragic, slow burning, sweet, dark, nerdy, chaste, fantastical. I loved the romance of Song of Songs and that one parking lot scene in *Sixteen Candles*. I considered the act of falling in love a holy act only bequeathed upon the blessed. I nursed a series of unrequited crushes on varsity basketball players. I volunteered to make my high school's Val-o-Grams and spent much of my early twenties lost in a cloud of romantic daydream.

My longest love story, the love story that precedes me and will follow me, is my Black romance, which is falling in love with my unique Black existence. The population of Black people in most sections of Orange County, California, where I was raised, hovers around 1.5 percent. When we first moved to our Orange County neighborhood in the early 1990s, we received letters with the words "nigger children" in them and my mom's van was coated with egg yolk on more than one occasion. I was often the only Black friend of anyone who wasn't Black themselves. The Black students at my school were mostly Black American with a smattering of first-generation African and Caribbean kids. Even if we didn't frequent the same social circles, all of us knew of each other. Alas, this fact did not prevent white teachers from mistaking us for one another.

My best friend during my freshman year in high school was Tamia. She was fair-skinned enough that strangers often asked if she was mixed, with curly hair that hung past her shoulder blades. She was smart, driven, and spoke my love language of sarcasm perfectly. We wrote each other letters about our crushes, talked shit about the crazy white girls, and debated on the artistry of the recent Destiny's Child video. Tamia came from a line of Great Migration, debutante balls, Black associations, and service to the community. I come from a line of egusi soup, the Protestant religion, and a first-generation push to become lawyer/doctor/engineer or perish. Tamia and I were from different parts of the Black pool, but this fact never troubled our friendship.

Unfortunately, Tamia was close friends with a girl named Monique, who was blatantly territorial and didn't like me very much. It was public knowledge I had a crush on her ex-boyfriend, a point guard with a round, high butt and ridiculous dimples. Her favorite form of social attack was about my supposed Oreo-ness. She was fond of telling me that I *spoke funny* and that my alternative fashion choices—in the early millennium, I went through a phase of emo cut-up T-shirts and wearing a combination of lip gloss and mascara to create black lipstick—were peak wannabe.

Her comments hit my little Black heart with a pang. Prior to high school, my social ties were formed within the tribe of the Suburban White Girl. My mixed assimilation desires granted me conditional entry, though my trial period never seemed to end. I studied the customs of salads at lunch, highlights, and an adoration for thigh gaps. I listened to their crushes on skater boys with names like Garret and Skylar.

I was out of place in these social groups but often felt just as discordant when I sought companionship based on color alone. Because I was raised by a white woman for the first four years of my life, loved Third Eye Blind more than Nelly, and would rather read *Catcher in the Rye* than *Native Son*, I occasionally wondered if my cultural departures were secretly some sign I hated myself. I'd hear some well-meaning friend make a declaration about what was Black and what was not, and I didn't fit the mold. I also felt distant from the more prevalent Black American experience and the Nigerian experience. I was a first-generation Californian who could look over her shoulder and catch The Continent.

Black culture across the diaspora thrives in part because of an ubuntu "I am because we are" communal sway. Our survival has been predicated on cohesion. Sometimes, in efforts to uphold *group* identity, our individuality can easily slide from simple difference to your group membership being relentlessly questioned. I am not the only Black person who has been accused (and it so often feels like an accusation) of "acting white" simply when my action differed from what was considered to be standard.

In another universe, Monique's petty bullying would have been harmless teenage asides that I would have shrugged off or spat back at her. But in my high school social context, when I was so deeply invested in *coolness* and already laced with an accumulation of "not Black enough" papercuts, her interpretation that I was an Oreo landed like truth. It was decided: I needed to become more Black. Me—the dark-skinned African girl who even in high school resembled an extra from *The Woman King*. Me, with my thick braids and roots that stretch from Benin to Nigeria. I needed to become more Black.

But how?

My first stop was to sharpen up my communication, to speak the language. While I could *understand* various African diasporic languages to include most variations of AAVE, I was not exactly proficient on a speaking level. I had been told that I talked like a white girl since kindergarten.

I ventured to urbandictionary.com to browse appropriate slang, sure to cause Monique to experience deep pangs of regret that she ever thought to try me. The next day at school, at break time, we were heading to the upper commons to buy some chili cheese fries. I waited for the perfect break in conversation to deploy my linguistic arsenal. I had my chosen word—which

I believed to be legit because I may have heard it in *Save the Last Dance*, a cinematic portrait of actual urban life—and I listened for the perfect moment to drop it. In a break in the conversation between Tamia and Monique about some party, that I probably couldn't go to anyways because my African parents barely let me go anywhere that wasn't basketball or school related, I say my word.

To this day, an almost dissociative pink fog overtakes my senses when I try to recall the exact word I used. It's as if my brain knows I cannot take the embarrassment even now and intervenes. I think I may have said, "Get it gully," but the fact was that Tamia and Monique looked at me like I had suddenly grown an eye in the middle of my forehead. From that chili-cheese-fry day onward, I decided that faking it was never going to be my lane—if I were going to fall in love with the exact kind of Blackness I was, I had to accept all of me; this is true love.

I believe this quest, this of honoring the specificity of my Black story within the diaspora, is a grand romance, an adventure deserving a happy ending without ever uttering the words "get it gully" aloud. It is for this reason that I am an afro-romantic.

Working Definitions

> **Afro-romantic:** An attitude that holds that Blackness is a love story stretching across space and time.
> **Articulations:** A way to speak, to sound out, to e-nun-ci-ate as to be understood by another (even if that Other is Self).

The Afro-Romantic as Survival of the Chillest[23]

I like being Black. Even during times when being the daughter of Black immigrants feels like a tightrope, when the space between African American

---

23 The naming convention for this chapter of afro-romanticism is an emulation of Carmen Maria Machado's memoir *In the Dream House* (Graywolf Press, 2019).

lingers wide as a planet, I like being Black. Afro-romantic is a reminder that Black is just another word for human. I am an afro-romantic and my slogan is very chill: I like being Black.

The Afro-Romantic as Pangea

My grandmother would have rather I married a white man than an Igbo one. This fact is ridiculous but then again, so is tribalism. The African diaspora is a real life Pangea, a fused land mass that drifted into the separate continents of Africa and Asia and South America and the other continents we know today after a series of massive shakes. There was a time, before words and associations, that this entire planet was Black. The afro-romantic accepts the union and separations inherent to Blackness.[24]

I hold the privilege of knowing, without DNA test, that I am Yoruba by way of Nigeria. This proximity to my roots is not a gift I take lightly. I've heard the stories of first-generation Africans arrogantly separating themselves from Blackness. I have experienced misplaced hostility as soon as someone who is Black American or Caribbean American learns that I am Nigerian. I know these new and old tribal anxieties will not be solved overnight, and I have zero desire to win the Good Black, the Better Black, the Real Black contest. I've heard the prizes suck.

---

24 Yoruba thought considers *orí*, or head, to be where the spiritual destiny of an individual is stored. When I was in Nigeria in 2016, I had the honor of meeting with Baba Elebuibon, one of the preeminent Ifá priests. Hailing from Osogbo, Òsun State, Elebuibon has key ties to Òsun due to his family lineage's history and Òsun's presence in the town as a patron deity. A family's orí might be reflective in the family name or even closely related to a particular orisa. A last name like Ogunnaike might mean that this particular family was once a part of a clan or *egbe* related to the male deity of metalwork, Ogun. As the Yoruba tradition migrated, understandings of orí became much more personal. An individual was said to house the energy or patterns of a certain orisa, even as they might still be a part of a particular spiritual family. Destiny is encapsulated within one's *orí inu*, or inner head. While every human is thought to have free will, each soul is said to choose their life's circumstances, to include parents, stresses, and crises as opportunities to grow. (Some of us are shaking our heads like WTF were our pre-baby primordial selves thinking right about now.) When we think of our work on this earthly plane, it can be helpful to think of both our individual and collective destinies as being intertwined, neither more important than the other. This too is afro-romantic.

Tribal formations and the mistrust they often spawn are nothing new to my afro-romance. We've been doing this for a while. Yoruba people are a combination of several tribal identities including but not limited to the Ondo, Ijesa, Oyo, and Egba.[25] Yoruba people are both a dilution and a union of the old Oyo Empire—and there are still separations today. My mother and father both grew up in Yorubaland, a borderless expanse that stretches across southwestern Nigeria, into Benin, and further into Togo, which was colonized by British, French, and German interests ignorant of tribal affiliation. And though they share a very distinct tribe, they each speak totally different dialects of Yoruba that are mostly indecipherable to the other.

Afro-romantics know that healing tribal mistrust is no smooth enterprise. There is nothing as easily defeated as a house divided. While Blackness is currently separated by mindset, spirituality, region, education, class, gender, immigration status, Pangea will arrive again. The African diasporic migration, from together, to separate, to together, is the movement of humanity overall, a messy, earthquake bound journey towards a supercontinent of love.

The Afro-Romantic as American Girl Doll

My youngest brother read *The Autobiography of Malcolm X* when he was twelve. He may have been the only Pan-Africanist middle schooler in Orange County. He decided he wanted to change his last name to X in honor of *his people*. My father had to explain to him that Eko was not the white man's name.

I know it may sound strange, but I was a little disappointed when I learned that I was not the direct descendant of enslaved people.[26] I was in

25 Olatunde B. Lawuyi and Obafemi Arowolo, "The Reality and Meaning of Being a Woman in the Yoruba Cosmogonic Myths," *An Anthopologist's Contributions to O. Gbadegesin's 'Destiny, Personality, and the Ultimate Reality and Meaning of Human Existence: A Yoruba Perspective*, URAM, 7: 173–188, University, Ile-Ife, Nigeria.

26 In 1927, Zora Neale Hurston sat down with Cudjoe Lewis, the last known living survivor of the Middle Passage, for a series of interviews. The resulting nonfiction work was presented almost entirely in dialect and bridged the experiences of Lewis's life, from being captured as a young man by the legendary Dahomey army (an army made notorious because of their fierce

fourth grade and loved nothing more than rooting for the underdog. But somehow in that two-day Civil War lesson, I deduced that my Blackness had a different origin story. In fourth grade, I was also deeply invested (read: obsessed) about the American Girl franchise, a book and doll series detailing historical eras through the adventures of girls. I loved Samantha Parkington and Addy Walker the most: Samantha (the Edwardian era doll) because she had the best clothes, and Addy because she had the best heart (though, I did love the pink pinafore and cowrie necklace).

Some parents were angry that the only Black American doll (at the time), Addy, was enslaved and spent much of the book series contending with this legacy. Addy was the first American Girl doll to have an advisory board (made up of an impressive cadre of Black thought leaders, professional artists, and historians). There was a lot of loving care that went into the making of this doll, from the style of her clothes (she was the first doll to wear earrings) to the intricacies of plantation life.

Addy's coming of age on a South Carolina plantation were brutal. She did not know her birthday and chose April 9. She looked up to her older brother Sam and loved her mother, father, and little sister Esther. Addy was spirited and kind and hopeful. Sometimes, I don't understand how. She was forced to understand cruelties that could break the most formidable adult. I will never forget when she was punished for daydreaming and forced to eat a juicy, green worm or when her brother and father were sold away. I will never forget her scary night escape to freedom and how her high hopes were constantly being crushed.

---

cadre of female warriors, sometimes called the "Dahomey Amazons") to co-founder of African-town, Alabama, a community for formerly enslaved people. Hurston's work was not published until 2018, due to publishers who were apathetic towards the book's subject matter and faithful rendering of Cudjo's dialect, but serves as yet another powerful rebuttal to unfinished stories of Africa: "Incomplete and romanticized readings of history have resulted in a fanatical, monolithic image of Africa, or worse, a dismissal of the continent as a backwards land that colonizers rightfully raided. Both myopic narratives prevent people from exploring the continent's full range of societies—not only spurring resentment among African Americans and African and Caribbean immigrants, but also promoting ignorance of the shared cultural elements that survived the journey across the Atlantic" (Torry Threadcraft, "The Power of Untold Slave Narratives," *The Atlantic*, October 1, 2018).

Addy was named for her great-grandmother. Slavery stole this privilege away from millions, and today we see Black people reclaiming this right. In the Yoruba tradition, after the seventh day of life, the newborn baby is christened with many names meant to concentrate your family destiny. A child who was hard won for might be named "Oluwabunmi" meaning "God gave you to me." Or "Babatunde," to honor a recently departed father, Babatunde meaning, "the father returns." One of the names given is your *oriki*; this is the name that marks you as belonging to a certain family history, the pet name your mom might call you when she was in a good mood.

When I found out that Addy was descended from the Yoruba people, I was at my parent's convenience store. For most of elementary school, my parents co-managed a mini market and laundry in Long Beach. I ran up to my mother at the register, pointing to the page like I won the lottery. Addy is short for Aduke, the *oriki* name we both share. I am an afro-romantic because "Aduke" means "much loved." Addy was a bridge, a way that I could accept all parts of me—the Nigerian, the Yoruba, the Black, the American. There was always a thread, even across a river of heartbreaks, somewhere.

The Afro-Romantic as You

And now comes the final stage of this epic romance: you. A stunning contradiction is always at play with the afro-romantic. We are individuals, yet never removed from the whole.[27]

---

27 "If there were a catastrophe which destroyed the rest of the world's population, most of the genetic variability in the world would still be present in sub-Saharan Africans" (California Newsreel, *Race—the Power of an Illusion*: Episode 1, "The Differences Between Us" Vimeo, July 15, 2015, vimeo.com/133506632.). In Toni Morrison's only short story, "Recitatif," she purposely keeps the race of her two female characters hidden. As readers, we are on the lookout for how easily and automatically we "race" characters, an obsession that often follows in real life. Race-ing people is one of the tricky and tricking portions of an essentialism, even a strategic one (shout out to Gayatri Chakravorty Spivak). We live in a world where race isn't real, but racism is. If we become too tied to essentialist arguments regarding race, we negate the complexity of our very human experience and further the work of racism. Scientists are still on a mad hunt to discover differences in humans according to race. Unfortunately for them, there is no sign that this search will be rewarded, and these scientists may very well join their eugenicist predecessors who measured skulls for intelligence.

There are approximately one to two billion Black bodies in this world currently, all perfectly expressing themselves. We have fissures; our togetherness snakes together, sharply diverges, comes cheek to cheek. We have fled from each other and have run into each other across continents and space and time. We will find our own Pangea exactly when we are ready to. Afro-romance is a union of difference, a practical love.

Thank you for making me an afro-romantic. Thank you for being Black exactly as you are. There is peace in your Blackness. Your story is an opportunity for true love. There is no greater romance than this. I love being Black because of you.

HONEYKNIFE PRAXIS

- **Drip:** Go on a Google rabbit hole journey about someone Black who inspires you.
- **Drizzle:** Write a love letter to your distinct Black lineage—the hurts, the meetcutes, the desires you are scared to name aloud.
- **Pour:** Release the haters. Hang out with people who like and accept you exactly as you are and for whom you feel the same and for whom you'd never have to use Urban Dictionary to impress.

8

Black Madonna of the Fretful Heart

I am not Catholic, and yet when I was in second grade and discovered a rain-stained Catholic prayerbook in my family's laundromat, I taught myself the Hail Mary. I was especially captured by the phrase "fruit of your womb" though I had absolutely zero idea what it meant.

My favorite story during my wannabe Catholic era is the *Le Jongleur de Notre Dame*,[28] about a socio-economically challenged juggler turned monk. The monk could not sing or dance or read very well, like the other monks, and his juggling was the only gift he could offer. One night, the other monks caught him on his knees—juggling and sweating bullets before the statue of the Great Mary. The monks were furious with the juggler's disrespect and moved to stop his sacrilegious act. But, before they reached him, they were stopped in their tracks. The Virgin Mary came to life, and, instead of condemning the monk, she used the edge of her gown to wipe the sweat from the juggler's brow.

My family, like most Yoruba people I know, are Protestant, which to me felt kind of like Christianity without the confetti. If we were going to do this monotheism thing, shouldn't we at least go all out? Suffering Jesus on Crucifix. Fluffy white confirmation dresses. Stained-glass

---

28 Also called *Our Lady's Juggler*, the miracle story was first published by children's book author Violet Moore Higgins in 1917 (retrieved January 31, 2021, https://archive.org/details/TheLittle-Juggler).

windows spinning rainbows on pews. Riding the bus after school, I'd watch, transfixed, as my Mexican friends would stop whatever they were doing—gossiping, GameBoying, gazing into outer space—to coolly cross themselves whenever we rolled past the Our Lady of Guadalupe.

I was not a little jealous that my friends, many of them Mexican, Salvadoran, and Guatemalan and who were predominantly Catholic, had this olive-skinned goddess called Mary; that instead of only pulling her out every Christmas for "Silent Night" were solid enough in their adoration to screen print her entire face onto blankets. Growing up, I could never escape Creepy Surfer Jesus and his stunningly blank blue eyes. His face decorated the walls of almost every African church I stepped foot in. This Creepy Surfer Jesus seemed nice enough (that kind guy smile, those comfy robes), but even as a kid, I remember wondering why our Jesus didn't have a tan.

If you are suspecting why this early Catholic spiritual bypassing was happening, you will not be surprised to know that I was a nervous kid. My birth picture resembles a midlife alcoholic: surprised bloodshot eyes, wavy mouth of repressed shame, quizzical *who me?* expression like I just returned from a Las Vegas bender.

I think my parents took my quirks and sensitivity as willful defiance, another burden to their already overwhelmed lives, a future liability for my future as a Black woman in America. I learned early on that a quiet, easygoing girl was a less-hit or yelled-at girl, someone who teachers picked for Student of the Month. Since all Students of the Month received a Burger King lunch date, which meant a Whopper Jr. meal including a paper crown, a quiet, easygoing girl was what I became. Unfortunately, my nerves were a frazzle teetering on the edge of a cliff. And so, whenever I desired some pearl of peace, I recited the Hail Mary. The inner hum of the rosary was enough to quiet down my static and bring me back to earth.

As a child, I did not call what I felt *anxiety*. First off, no one really talked like that in the 1990s or even the early millennium. There weren't any hashtags or B-list celebrities "getting vulnerable" about their panic attacks or stage fright. Adults wrongfully labelled my tendency towards selective mutism and sweaty nervousness being "slow"; kids thought I was weird, which was right, but *still*. I was class president and varsity basketball player, so my anxiety was not so debilitating that it overshadowed my ambition, but inside I was a thing always falling.

Anxiety is defined as a "feeling of worry, nervousness, or unease, typically about an imminent event or something with an uncertain outcome" and "desire to do something, typically accompanied by unease."[29] My body is a bell struck too hard that will not cease its ringing, even when I'm like, *I get it, I am floating on a giant rock during the horror show of late-stage capitalism and I don't know when I'm going to die or what the meaning of life is, but can you just, please, chill for like four seconds?*

My body replies no (with terseness because she can be testy like that)—she does not want to chill.

If you are anxiety-prone and sensitive, please give yourself a nice, non-scary pat on the back. If you carry the physical evidence of anxiety—tight muscles, racing thoughts, digestive issues, flightiness, difficulty sitting still—the last thing you need is more critique. You are a brave human to live with so much ability to feel. I know anxiety has an effect on your relationships with self, boyfriends, carbohydrates, girlfriends, your family, your job. I know how much you sometimes wish your anxiety did not exist.

Whether your anxiety is acute, moderate, or severe, I know the crushing feeling of dreaming so big but being overcome by nervousness that prevents you from taking even one step forward. I know how it feels to question your confidence and courage because of being overwhelmed. You're intelligent and practiced enough to know that your reaction is an over-response, but your WebMD knowledge and vinyasa excursions do not mean that your anxiety disappears.

Your body carries many beautiful inheritances that cannot be divorced

---

29 Oxford's English Dictionaries via Google search, 2020.

from your ancestors and *their* relationship to anxiety. The anxiousness you feel is wide. If your loved ones have an issue accepting their own fear, it usually follows that they are not great at handling yours. If you descend from people who have faced war, displacement, and violence (which is basically a part of all human history on earth), then your instincts will heighten. Your anxiety did not start with you and does not end with you. There are many things to be anxious about. I won't name them because, like most anxious people, you already know.

Your anxiety is in conversation with your world. I use those daily meditation and affirmation books quite a bit to start my day. In a world that abuses Black women's power for fun, repeating soothing sentences like "I am safe" or "The world loves me" sometimes feels like an exercise in How to Be Delusional 101.

During the summer of 2018, I was awarded a week-long summer fellowship in Italy to study the Black Madonna, a dark-skinned version of the Virgin Mary who decorated many shrines around the world, but especially in France, Italy, Poland, and Spain.[30] I was in grad school

---

30 "Examples of the Black Madonna may be found all over the world. According to some estimates, there are around 500 Black Madonnas in Europe alone, mostly Byzantine icons and statues in Catholic and Orthodox countries. A monastery in the city of Czestochowa in southern Poland, for instance, contains a dark-skinned Byzantine icon of the Holy Virgin. Meanwhile, a shrine in Einsiedeln Abbey, a Benedictine monastery around 25 miles (40km) southeast of Zurich in Switzerland, boasts a miraculous Black Madonna statue, its skin possibly darkened from centuries of exposure to candle smoke. Gates has also encountered a Black Madonna in a Greek Orthodox monastery on the island of Heybeliada, near Istanbul." (From Alastair Sooke's "The Intriguing History of the 'Black Madonna," *BBC*, July 19, 2018). Now, while it is heartening to know that Black womanhood is such a powerful visceral yearn that she arrives in European territory (not exactly lands known for their loving embrace of African femaleness) to be worshipped, I know that I must accept Her presence here as more bridge than final resting place. Any worship that flatly ignores colonization, racism, sexism, chattel slavery, and what this has done to Black women by proximity is half-baked love, a bouquet of red roses after a bitch slap. Africa is home to the original Black Goddess, but I love how well-traveled She is—crossing rivers, lakes, and oceans to soothe those who need her. Black Madonna shrines are in the most beautiful, pedestrian-averse places! Cliffs, hillsides, mountains—arriving to worship the Black Madonna is no simple straightforward feat. Some of her worshipers take weeks and days to find Her. Never simplify access to yourself. You are worthy of investigation, seduction, and care. The right ones, the ones who really want to give to you, will take the time and care to journey to your heart.

in Pittsburgh and I could not wait to make this trip. The plan was to document the fascinating juxtapositions of the Black woman in Italy, the fallacy of the Madonna/Whore dichotomy in a darker shade. I would study the thousands of female African migrants (many of whom originate from Benin City) who made the dangerous trek to Italy via Libya, searching for economic opportunity—women involved in a complicated sex trafficking trade where there were no clear victims or perpetrators. I would visit the Black Madonnas of Tindari and Positano, both of which have attracted significant, almost cult-like attention over hundreds of years.

While never worshipped as a standalone god because the patriarchy loves nothing more than to cockblock female spiritual authority, the Black Madonna has been a distinctly European phenomenon within the Christian church since at least the early fourteenth century. Scholars are divided as to whether the Black Madonna's dark skin—and the resulting reverence—is accidental or intentional. Some believe her face has been darkened over time through natural causes; some believe she is the descendant of African goddesses like Isis.

I was excited to visit Italy—land of Gucci, fettucine, and really hot men with romance-novel-like names (what girl doesn't want to hook up with a Fabrizio?), but of course I was nervous too. There are a number of Black women who have been flocking to Italy to experience the sweet life and find their own sweet husband. I know of Black woman artists who blossomed in Italy, finally free to experience their womanhood. I have a cousin, cute and big-eyed and innocent looking, who majored in Italian and spent some months studying abroad, who was chased and catcalled so much during her Italian trip that on her last day in Milan, an ending most of us would lament, she took a photo of herself doing an ecstatic jig.

Also, right before my trip to the beautiful country, I kept seeing butterflies. Seeing butterflies is hardly surprising in the thick of pre-summer in Pittsburgh, but they appeared to me within tattoos, bus ads, random stories sent by friends. My anxious mind loves nothing more than assigning meaning to random events, so off to Google I went with my question

113

about the butterfly sightings. I tried to find a New Age website that looked the most *legit* and scholarly. (Basically, any that did not announce itself with a lilac bubble font.) "Change," the Internet told me. "Seeing butterflies means a transformation is afoot." I was preparing to travel to a country I'd never been to while shifting through a breakup and finishing up my last full summer in grad school. "Well, duh," I replied to the Internet. "Yeah, okay," the Internet replied. "But did you also know that seeing butterflies means death?"

I wanted to be that Ecstatic Black Woman Nomad, replete in primary colors, sipping Moscato, seated on an infinity pool with her #blackexcellence crew. Instead, my mind was filled with potential scenarios of plane crashes and Vespa collisions. But, my tickets were bought and my Airbnbs were secured. And there was no way I was about to lose out on those security deposits. Death or not, I was going to Italy. Only time would tell whether my trip would be *Eat, Pray, Love* or *Final Destination*.

There's a story about the Black Madonna of Tindari[31] that I like. It's about a frantic mother desperate to heal her very sick baby daughter. We never learn the nature of the girl's illness, only that she is not doing too hot. In the story about the Black Madonna, not even the most famous doctor of the land has been able to cure the poor baby. But the woman's friends know a secret and testify to the power of the Black Madonna. The woman prays a prayer from the darkest, deepest part of her being to this Black Madonna asking for her daughter to be well. Some days later, the baby girl is completely healed.

Since the woman is overjoyed that her daughter escaped death's door, she decides to offer thanks to the Madonna of Tindari in person. The journey is wild, but they finally arrive to the site of the Black Madonna, ready to offer their thanks. Unfortunately, the woman is aghast when she *sees* the Madonna of Tindari. She expected a goddess who looked more like

---

31 From Obiettivo Mediterraneo's *Tindari: Cult and History*, 2015.

Marilyn Monroe, a burst of light. But this Madonna is Black,[32] serious, and small, with an inscription of *Nigra Sum Sed Formosa*, Latin for *I am black but beautiful*, decorating her.

The woman, who was once ready to praise the Black Madonna, is now angry and in complete disbelief that it is to *this* Black Madonna she had offered her thanks. *How can this Black Madonna be the thing that saved my daughter when she looks worse than me?* she thinks.

The woman is about to exit stage left, but alas, her daughter is nowhere to be found. The Church of the Madonna of Tindari is on a cliff, overlooking a twinkling cerulean sea. The mother feels queasy with fear. She has a feeling of where her baby girl was. Unable to look over the cliff, the woman rushes back into the church, falls on her knees before the same Madonna of Tindari she just hated on. She asks for forgiveness and prays for rescue. Hot holy tears rush down her face, wetting her blouse clean and through.

The woman's cries are so loud, she *almost* doesn't hear the laughter coming from over the cliff. Not having time to even wipe her face, the woman runs outside towards the noise. And there she sees her daughter, not dead but safe and sound. The townspeople said the sea receded right before the baby daughter landed and was discovered by a group of sailors. She even had the nerve to be playing with seashells. The woman falls to her knees, praising the Black Madonna of Tindari, kissing her forehead to the pebbled ground that almost claimed her own daughter.

Your anxiety may feel like a hum or a roar, but within that storm is a fight between your want and need, your outward-facing self and your

---

32 "Sanctuaries that feature Black Madonnas have long been among the most popular pilgrimage destinations for Christians. The very darkness, or better said, non-whiteness, of their venerable Marian icons disrupts facile interpretations and raises challenging questions that revolve around the icons' origins, potency, and meaning." Jeanette Favrot Peterson, *Visualizing Guadalupe: From the Black Madonna to the Queen of the Americas* (University of Texas Press, 2014). Instead of a hybridization of spiritualities, early Christian missionaries demeaned and erased the Indigenous practices they found, upheld their own reflection (white, male, war hungry, exacting) as the sole image of God. The Black Madonna is a curious comma in this enterprise.

inner truth. You could picture the woman, the mother in this tale, as the part of you that is desperate for repair. The sick baby girl is your most vulnerable, naked self, the most tender part of your soul. And the Black Madonna is the part of you that seeks to protect this tenderness.

We all have a baby girl inside, a young bundle of energy still so vulnerable to harm that she needs a mother to survive. We also have a mother inside, a powerful nurturing and wise presence that wants us to live without fear. How our own inner mother responds to the baby girl of our soul depends on so many overlapping factors. Are we subsisting on four hours of sleep? Are we surrounded by gossip and petty drama? How we seek care for our more vulnerable needs has everything to do with how much we have to give. In this story, the mother was present enough to know her vulnerable self needed help and was brave enough to seek it. She trusts her friends, who want the best for her baby daughter. She offers a deep prayer on faith because she knows her baby girl deserves life.

Many of us instinctively want relief from our anxiety. Anxiety can be exhausting and extremely tough to deal with. And so we seek help. Zoloft. Shein shopping sprees. Plantain. Sometimes *how* we seek is more important than *what* we are seeking. Something shifts when we take action from a more steady, loving aspect of ourselves instead of our straight terror.

The second miracle of the Tindari tale is when the woman comes to face to face with the Black goddess. You know how you spend a couple thousand lifetimes believing that some great, rich, skinny, famous, miracle cure will defeat that brutal hum of fear always at the corner of your mind?

The Black Madonna is a physical reminder of what the woman disowned: her deep, dark, ancient self. It was not some colossal goddess of light who performed the miracle for the woman in the Tindari tale, some diamond-plated statue that instantly made the woman genuflect.

It was this small thing, this dark thing, this old thing.

This still holy thing.

Refusing to behold the true savior of her baby girl, the woman loses sight of the most vulnerable part of herself so completely that she lets her poor baby fall off a cliff. There is a power in our humility when we can stop playing brave and can acknowledge how terrified we are sometimes. How freeing it is to slip off the performance and quiet the job of being never-scared. There is so much we do not control. Anxiety teaches us this. How rude she is, erupting when we are at work meeting or on a first date. She does not care for anything but the truth.

Only when you bow to the holiness and immense beauty of your body's wise anxiety can your full vitality be restored. Without her protection, there is no baby girl.

Your inner Black Madonna is generous. She not only rescues your vulnerability time and time again with her deep, dark, ancient power, but when you acknowledge her, she will move oceans for your safe landing. She even gives your tenderness a plaything, a toy of protection—a shell.

Your fear is a healthy generational defense, which has saved your life and saved your people. We like to talk a lot about the lofty, courageous deeds of our people. That is very well, but fear also has helped someone escape a predator or sense when war was approaching. When you can allow this feeling to just be instead of fighting the reality of your stomach and your heartbeat, you become free. This freedom is the result of your sweet acceptance. If you are sensitive, you are probably also pretty sensitive to the experience of anxiety. This may be a particular bane for you and cause you to constantly police your anxiety, to compare yourself to friends who seem stoic and chill. Maybe your baby girl soul is more sensitive, and this is just what it is. I hope you can accept this. I hope your rebuke thaws into gentle reverence.

More prehistoric than water, your desire for safety and comfort has saved the most tender part of you for millions of years. And as annoying as it may be, it is your anxiety that is saving you now.

I did not die in Italy—not straightaway anyways. I landed in Catania easily and slept overnight in an airport hotel. The next morning, I took a three-hour car ride to a town near Tindari, home of the Black Madonna.

The driver was kind. He offered me small peach candies that I overate and spent most of the ride telling me how pretty I was with a lavish enthusiasm that equally delighted and made me wonder if he was taking me to an underground brothel. In Tindari, the host family of the Airbnb took great pains to make me feel welcome, to the point of securing a personal driver to the Black Madonna and taking me out until two in the morning to this night market thing, gently urging me to try *arancini*.

Sitting around a table, rice ball in mouth with kindly Italians at an evening market cafe, I felt sadness at how limiting my anxiety was. I could barely enjoy myself; my nerves were still operating at high octane. I knew I shouldn't be this stressed out. Clearly in this instance, I could posit that the Universe did indeed *have my back* or whatever. But my body? The roving percolation of my nerves? Absolutely, not.

The next day, I arrived at the Sanctuary of the Madonna of Tindari mid-morning, alongside hundreds of visitors. Some say the white sand circling below the church resembles the profile of the Madonna herself, holding a baby.

An international gaggle of tourists milled outside, posing for selfies on the steps. Inside, the church was cool like the tips of a shadow and darkly lit by the brightness filtering in through stained glass of blue, pink, and yellow. Tired families lounged on pews and held cameras upwards to capture pictures of the domed ceiling, which is painted with a rendition of the Madonna and the village of Tindari. I lit a candle, said a micro prayer, and sat down.

The statue of the Black Madonna perched calmly at the very end of the aisle, lifted in the air by seraphim. Gold columns surrounded her, and I was surprised at how small she was, how closely I had to walk to her to get a good but still grainy photo. She was straight-mouthed and the color of wet soil—black-brown midnight. I couldn't tell if she were happy to be there, but she didn't seem too disturbed. The church was a murmur of low conversation, clicking phones, scattered child steps.

Sitting in the pew, the familiar drone of the "Hail Mary" began. My head bowed and my eyes closed to the lullaby of comfort. *Hail Mary, Mother of God, the Lord be with you. Blessed you are among women, and blessed is the fruit of your womb, Jesus.*

There is peace in my anxiety. My anxiousness is one place I meet my most honest self. And if I were ever going to find a peace that lasted longer than the latest mediator—be it yoga, journaling, or even speaking to a therapist—I was going to have to sit with the death my fear was trying to outrun. I was going to have to sit still enough to feel the holiness of my fear.

Here is how. There is a story of a Black woman who departed the safety of the Black Madonna of Tindari. After a day's rest, she hopped on a morning train to the capital of Sicily. It is the year of our Goddess summer 2018. She goes on several dates with hot Italian men. Some are romantic. Some are not. She samples pistachio gelato and has a two-hour conversation with an Australian expat. In Palermo, she plans to visit an all-Black exhibit called *Resignifications: The Black Mediterranean,* an art display honoring the voids and violences surrounding African Diasporic art.

She walks through the streets of this ancient city, wearing a bodycon cotton dress in red, white, and blue and wishing she had worn something less obviously American tourist. Her thighs rub together and pine for spandex. She is hopelessly lost. The street signs are difficult, melting into each other, missing in some places. Her body is a familiar buzz of static that makes it hard to think. Pregnant grey clouds move in on the horizon. Eggplant-skinned men sell bags on the street, and rust tear stains run down the front of churches. She focuses on the doors of peeling paint and the fashionable women strutting in oversized sunglasses.

Palermo is a dizzying, electric fusion of cultures—from Arabic to Greek. This woman falls in love with Palermo for its proud contradiction, the ocean, the mighty chested mountains. When this woman was a girl, she had taught herself the Hail Mary and loved the story *Le Jongleur de Notre Dame.* Lost in Palermo, trying to reach *Resignifications,* and having yet another anxiety attack, the woman breathes into the space of her own offering, her own truth. A thought breaks through

119

her familiar fear, like a ship in dense fog, simple and brief:

You are still alive.

The woman stops trying to be a woman who does not live with anxiety. She stops trying to put on a stoic face of nonchalance. She inhales. She thanks the manifestation of her small, dark, plain self. Her anxiety is her protector, doing its best to shield her from harm. Her Black Madonna is the sweat trickling down her temples, the heavy safeguard locking her solar plexus, the tight ribbon of her shoulders. This is her armor, her shield.

For some moments, she slows down enough to hear the language of her fear. She realizes her anxiety is not her fault, is not *a* fault, and that this feeling will not kill her. She breathes, deep and slow and sure. She luxuriates in the uncertainty of life that arrives between pauses and how little she will ever really know of what comes after.

Her anxiety melts into something less sharp, and her thoughts become clear things. The woman finally finds her way to the exhibit thanks to the kind intervention of strangers and her busted Italian. The sound of thunder echoes closer, rumbling like a reminder. She enters the broad, quiet art space, and the sky finally opens its mouth, pounding the roof with rain.

HONEYKNIFE PRAXIS

- **Drip:** Practice pausing throughout your day, especially before transitional points—entering a new venue, ending a call, placing an order.
- **Drizzle:** Begin a daily meditation practice. Five minutes is more than fine to start.
- **Pour:** Attend or create your own ten-day silent meditation retreat. Don't be surprised if ancient Eminem songs play on repeat in your head.

9

Bitter Bees

The year is 2005 and somehow, I get my hands on a leaked mixtape track called "It Wasn't You" by Nas featuring Lauryn Hill. The pair hasn't released a single since their 1996 hit "If I Ruled the World." "It Wasn't You" is a storytelling opus that features Nas in tiptop form rapping about a romantic liaison between his lyrical self and a mysterious woman, the kind of woman who many rappers of that era immortalized in their songs. Lest Black girls forget the Kardashianistic mulatto phenotype rappers prefer, we are even introduced to her dimensions precisely: "Hair, black and long, Indian skin complexion / Eyes, nose and lips resemble the Egyptian." Still, I play the song on repeat, lullabied to sleep listening to Lauryn Hill's desire echoing lonely across the chorus.

I am a first year RAT at New Mexico Military Institute, located in the alien capital of the world: Roswell, New Mexico. RAT is short for recruit-at-training, a very intentional acronym used to denote our placement in the military school hierarchy. NMMI bills itself as the West Point of the West and is half high school/half junior college, full of future service academy cadets, ROTC trainees, juvenile criminal offenders, and rich kids whose parents wanted their children to enjoy a highly repressed secondary school experience. (I still count Roswell as one of the strangest years of my life and I hope my brother Jr. can forgive me, for he also ended up spending one year at NMMI.)

My friend Chanel and I are at NMMI as preps—we will spend one year here preparing for the technical and military rigors of the Coast Guard

Academy and the US Merchant Marine Academy, respectively. One day Chanel will become a helicopter pilot and fly over me in Tampa Bay as I, a thirty-something, wave like an excitable three-year-old child seeing planes for the first time.

But this day, in 2005, I am with my usual group of delinquent girl cadets in our barracks. We are ditching weekly marching practice to watch *Oprah* on low volume. The blinds are drawn to misdirect troop commanders. At a school chockfull of rigid expectations and regimented schedules, TV is a much needed reprieve. We have made up excuses or outright lies for our absences: last minute meeting with chem professor; sweettalking a troop commander with a crush; cramps.

Chanel serves as de facto leader (holder of the remote). We look up to Chanel because she is a mature twenty to our eighteen and has already survived Coast Guard basic training. She's practically an elder.

Suddenly, the TV with Oprah presiding over her middle-America kingdom goes black.

"What the hell?" we chirp immediately like baby birds. We look around in scattered anxiety as to who turned the TV off.

And Chanel is just like, "Say 'Thank you, Wyclef.'"

We laugh because no one takes Chanel's request seriously. She doesn't appear to be high nor were any of us presently discussing Wyclef or *any* other member of the Fugees at that precise moment, so we assume that Chanel is joking. We ask her to turn on the TV, but Chanel is adamant. "Say, 'Thank you, Wyclef,'" she says again.

And so, because we want our Oprah, we oblige. We say these three words like bored preschoolers, rolling our eyes for good measure. And Chanel, true to her word, turns the TV back on.

"Why did you ask us to do that?" I ask her.

She stares straight ahead, thinking deep Zen-master thoughts. "Because if Wyclef hadn't broken Lauryn Hill's heart, *The Miseducation* would not exist."

No other explanation by the way. NMMI was very strange.

The Miseducation of Lauryn Hill is proof yet again that some of our glorious creations emerge from shit, especially when that compost is the sweet decomposition of love. Hill was writing about grief both intimate and political—the ways that Black women experience a world where our safety, autonomy, and care is largely invisible.

It never ceases to amaze me how many times I hear the word "bitter" lobbed towards Black women en masse, as if we were born with hardened shells. Of course, many of the pundits and Internet Famous personalities decrying the inherent bitterness of Black women never delve *too deeply* into why Black women may be bitter. In addition to being the word describing the opposite of sweet, bitter is an emotional state. Oxford Languages defines bitter when talking about people as "angry, hurt, or resentful because of one's bad experiences or a sense of unjust treatment." The Bitter Black Woman is often interchanged with the Angry Black Woman, that livid phantom of the American and wider world shadow. This collective disavowal of our complex emotional experience makes owning and moving through our resentment and yes, even our bitterness, a tricky path indeed.

I remained largely unscathed from the rough waters of romantic love. I was a socially awkward avoidant, preferring unrequited love affairs that solely existed in robust colorful sequence in my own head and falling "in love" (read: rabid infatuation) with deeply unavailable men. I was Queen of the Crushed, content to break my own heart before I allowed any man the honor. Also, I felt sort of invisible in the whole dating scene. My look (off-duty Amazon warrior[33]) was not exactly in hot demand during the

---

33 I've always had a soft spot for Amazons, ancient women warriors made famous in real time by the Dahomey Amazons, in popular culture with *Xena: Warrior Princess*, and every height fetish website I erroneously landed on surfing the internet, looking for longer jeans. In 2014, I graced a Washington, DC stage as Miss Tall International and issued an earnest nerdy speech about Amazons while dressed as Diana of Themyscira, otherwise known as Diana Prince, but most commonly known as Wonder Woman. Invented by William Moulton Marston in the 1940s as a feminine embodiment of strength, leadership, and wisdom, she graced the inaugural issue of Gloria Steinem's *Ms. Magazine* and has been a DC Comics hall of famer for almost a hundred years. Amazons, in their obvious display of toughness, speak deeply to their culture's relationship to feminine power: "The Amazon archetype appears to be highly mutable, and (contd.)

mid-aughts unfortunately, let alone my alternative tastes and interests. I blamed myself mostly. Maybe if I were prettier and not as tall. Maybe if I were light-skinned and into makeup as a second art. Maybe if I were more extroverted. Maybe, maybe, maybe.

We all have a Wyclef (or several): heartbreaking experiences that complicate our relationship to gratitude. These heartbreaking moments leave their mark in the form of adorable accessories like trust issues, scarcity consciousness, and general terror of intimacy. Naturally, we will not always feel grateful for our losses and our wounds, even as we know they also bring depth of spirit and compassion. These persistent griefs will not always "make us a better person," and yet many of us have had that well-meaning auntie or friend who tells us that we should "just be grateful." "It all happened for a reason" is offered as a grand and noble excuse of our pain, but this line of reasoning does not always suffice. It's like me punching you in the face, offering you some strawberry ice cream in trade, and wondering why you didn't say thank you.

Nowhere does this tension between gratitude and ingratitude flower into being more than in the realm of romance. Though there are some of us lucky enough to have experienced smooth-sailing love lives, the seas have been very choppy for many others. Black women face unique challenges when it comes to love: residential segregation, economic limits, harmful stereotypes, queerphobias, traditional families (which equate having a man to

---

easily interpreted according to the whims of subjective taste. The Amazon was an antisexual manhater, or she was an aggressive, demanding sex object. She served the system by emulating men, or she was a rebel expanding the meaning of femininity, a threat to patriarchy. She was a demeaning, impossible fabrication, or she was an uprising, revelator reality. She was objectified as fearful and repellent, glamorous and appealing; a destructive and negative role mode, or one that was suitable for all young girls. For many, the Amazon was a fascination, a fixation, a flirtation, to hate or admire." (J. A. Salmonson, *The Encyclopedia of Amazons: Women Warriors from Antiquity to the Modern Era*. New York: Open Road Integrated Media, 2015.) Even my home state California is Amazon inspired. Queen Calafia, a mythical Black Amazon queen, ruled over a tribe of gorgeous woman warriors within *The Adventures of Esplandián* written by Garci Rodríguez de Montalvo. The 1510 novel is said to have inspired California's name and countless early explorers of the "New World." In the novel, Calafia leaves her home and deserts her faith. Perhaps her story stands as both homage and warning to her Amazonian descendants, a testament to the allure of female power and efforts to control it.

the greatest prize a woman can attain). Instead of receiving compassion and assistance to de-center romantic love from our lives, we are told to improve ourselves into oblivion to finally be worthy of a Starbucks date. Romantic love is held up as the cherry on the ice cream sundae for a life well done.

I am not grateful for these romantic hardships, the personal and political. I am not jumping for joy for the years I spent worrying about becoming yet another high-achieving, romantically lonely Black woman. I am not cheered by Black woman romance statistics or how much less white women must struggle for equitable relationships. (Though, I must add, romantic disappointment is an equal-opportunity experience.) It sucks and it hurts and I am tired of pretending otherwise.

Perhaps you've read the studies about the power of gratitude, bought the gratitude journals, blessed your plate with rushed whispers of thanksgiving. Gratitude, a state of appreciation on the positive "unearned" aspects of your life, has been shown to have numerous benefits on mental and emotional health.[34] You may know that gratitude primes your senses to notice the good stuff, which means instead of getting stuck in Google holes about cancer symptoms and the statistical chances you'll meet a man of equal yoking, you go on a walk.

But, gratitude can be *weird*. It can feel forced, like pretending to really adore lima beans and acid rain. In America, ingratitude is close to treason. Conservative pundits talk about protesters as entitled *whiners* who should be on their knees (unless the "The Star-Spangled Banner" is playing, of course). There is a shaming aspect to much of modern-day self-help culture that equates dissatisfaction to bitterness.

Your boss thinks you should be grateful for crumbs of recognition instead of a raise. Your partner doesn't understand that listening is labor. And your own family may be quick to reply to your question of tradition with exhortations to "count your blessings." Everywhere you turn, you are being told to

---

34 M.E., McCullough, R.A., Emmons, and J. Tsang, "The Grateful Disposition: A Conceptual and Empirical Topography," *Journal of Personality and Social Psychology* 82, 112–127, 2002.

shut up, keep quiet, and "just say thank you."

This is especially true for those of us cosigned to the Bitter Black Woman pile. Instead of looking closely why and how we hurt, we are lumped into *having an attitude* or *just being jealous.* When Black women demand more and meet the tendrils of our want, we are accused of becoming a stuck-up bitch who needs to be taken down a peg. Or five hundred.

Your desire for more than what you have is not a pathology to be tamed; it is a conundrum to be worked with.

Our "troublesome desires" and our ingratitudes create our freedom. We were unwilling to settle for certain cancers being death sentences, for subpar education, for unequal treatment before the law. We wanted more. That wanting is why we have life-saving developments like chemotherapy, public school education, and Miranda rights—even as we have a ways to go before freedom really means free.

My romantic nadir co-occurred during my five years of military school. The most action I received was this ridiculously built football player absentmindedly placing his hand on my thigh for four seconds when we went bowling. The fact that I thought about what this action *meant* for weeks shows you how dire things were. I had a handful of crushes who always seemed to have crushes on girls who were my physical opposite. That my bad romance years were occurring at a school where men were in the ninetieth percentile and I was supposedly "in the prime of my life" did not exactly shore up my ego.

For about three months, I electively woke up at 4:45 a.m. to run miles with a gung-ho former Marine Corps sergeant who terrified half of the regiment and inspired cult-like love with the other half. Running around the same Long Island neighborhood that inspired F. Scott Fitzgerald to write *The Great Gatsby*, I imagined myself in whirlwind romances where a revolving door of handsome, sapiosexual men seduced me with cherry black roses and eternal promises of love.

The idealization of romance protected me in some ways. I could pretend away the constant ache of loneliness and buffer my fears that I would die a virgin. I am grateful for that in some ways. However, much these high standards also put me at a distance from the actual risks I needed to take if I wanted to love and be loved as much as I said I did—namely, actually talking to someone of the opposite sex without collapsing into a sweat puddle. My romantic era following military school was much kinder. After pouring out my heart on a LiveJournal about my lovelessness state, another user pointed out that maybe I should, you know, take some action besides word vomiting online. And so, your girl started her OkCupid. She fell in love, discovered the joys of cunnilingus, and realized that men were better and way worse than their romantic novelizations. She also realized that she did not need to wait for a man for anything.

Am I grateful for my protracted years of romantic loneliness? Sometimes yes, sometimes no. My self-protection left my heart soft but also greatly inexperienced in the real-life waves of love. Sometimes bitterness still arrives when I see the wide discrepancy between what Black women are expected to perform versus what my friends who are not Black receive for simply showing up. Gratitude can never be an exercise in "spinning" disadvantage into blessing, making it into some metaphysical PR move.

If you need to ignore any emotion to experience gratitude, you are not in gratitude—you are in denial. For your gratitude to be something with teeth, you must hold the bitter and the sweet—for, in the end, they are the same thing.

Many of us stuck in loops of ingratitude tend to notice the negative first because our brains want to survive another day. Our hypervigilance is a key to this endurance. But left uninterrogated, this lens becomes the default way we see the world. We are survivors, adept at scanning horizons for threats real and imagined. Our fears offer up countless ways our life is wrong and lacking, like some frenzied internal megaphone blaring out the same song: "Scarcity Ahead!"

When we welcome each experience as if it were a teacher, especially within the realm of our romantic lives, we are practicing a divine gift. We are doing more than making lemons out of lemonade; we are inventing a new fruit. We are holding our entire life. Gratitude is a cognitive trick, especially for those of us predisposed to noticing what's missing. Instead of performative thankfulness and put-on happiness, we sit with the rawness of what we feel even as we mine our experience for what it has provided us. Dialectical gratitude is when we thank our stuck habits, the shadow side we'd rather ignore, the ex who we thought would break us.

We are saying, "Thank you, heartbreak—that there was a heart to break."

Sometimes, all you can manage is gratitude for your ingratitude, for the ways your needs have been unfulfilled and for the audacity to demand more. Perhaps, the loss you have suffered can never be shifted into a grateful heart or become a bullet point on your gratitude list. Maybe your ingratitude tells a truth about your dignity. Or maybe your ingratitude is evidence that you aren't quite over it—and that's okay too.

Look at certain hardships in your life: your fear of commitment, your codependent habits, your shopping addiction. These are your Wyclefs. Chances are that, even at their most disastrous, they have given you *something*, even if it was only the ability to know yourself more truthfully. Something like closure arrives when we can really thank even these sore places for what they have provided.

A requirement of the US Merchant Marine Academy is three hundred sea-going days to graduate. We call it sea year, and it's one of the most exciting and stress-inducing parts of our time at the Academy. Each midshipman spends two separate assignments at sea collecting days, working on school projects, learning their own specialty, and trying to avoid seasickness.

My first sea year took me to Germany, the Netherlands, and London. My second sea year brought me to Alaska, the United Arab Emirates, the Philippines, and Kuwait. Sea year is tough for everyone, but can be especially hard for women cadets. There are horrible stories of sexual assault and harassment. A chief engineer decorated our entire computer room with softcore porn from the 1980s. One of my captains would occasionally walk around shirtless on deck, heading to the bow where all the containers were so he could shoot his pistol in peace. (His gun, not the other one.)

Ever the romantic, I could not help but dream about romance. I had crushes of course. An able-bodied seamen with sad, hazel eyes and cornrows. A third-mate old enough to be my father when I was nursing a serious zaddy need. An Army security enlisted dude who looked like he had climbed out of the pages of an Abercrombie & Fitch catalog. The most action I received during this time was when an engineer mistakenly knocked on my door when he was drunk.

But, the ocean is a lullaby. Sometimes at night, I would leave my cabin, walk to the stern of the ship, and gaze out. Most of the time, there was not a ship in sight, just millions of stars and a vast black ocean. I loved the immense gravity of these moments—how insignificant and important I felt all at once with nothing but miles of sea. Over the horizon were ships and people and stories, but leaning against the bulwark of the ship, wind whipping my face, it was just me and my desire. I was always grateful that even in the face of such loneliness, I dreamed of something more.

We feel out of sync when we are not honest about our desires and our gratitudes. Desires, even at their most extreme, like wanting a pink electric Benz or a villa in Tuscany, are simply truth. It does not matter if your desires are feasible, if they are socially acceptable, or whether you are "deserving" of them. Desires are like air and stars; desires simply *are*. And so, please don't let someone tell you what you should have wanted and should have been thankful for. Let your heart sing forward about what you really crave.

The same is also true for our gratitude: whether we acknowledge the gifts of our lives or not, they are present. When we ignore our desires and hyperfocus on gratitude, we suppress life-force energy and lie to ourselves. When we ignore our gratitude in favor of our desires, we will forever be a hungry ghost, always wanting, never full.

If we are to be in something like balance, our desires must loom as large as our gratitude. (This practice is especially crucial for those of us who just can't help but dream and desire big.)

Forget about worthiness and obligation.

Get real about what you want and what you have.

There is peace even in your dissatisfaction.

Your discontent is an inevitable stop on the road of gratitude.

The first time I saw Lauryn Hill was in the "Killing 'Em Softly" video on MTV. She was lovely and dark, wise-eyed and at ease in her brilliance. I immediately asked my mother if I could grow thick-fingered locs like her, believing part of her secret sauce must lie in her hair. Unsurprisingly, my mother said no. But when I started growing my own locs out, I thought of them as a late gift to that little girl sitting on her couch, nursing a contraband Coke and watching Lauryn Hill.

I've seen Lauryn Hill three times in concert from DC to NYC. I've faced the usual complaints that now haunt a Lauryn Hill performance: she's often hours late, and the songs are unrecognizable remixes. Sometimes I feel a longing for *our* Lauryn Hill. The Lauryn Hill belting in *Sister Act* or grinning with an armful of Grammy's. The one starring in indie features and gracing the cover of *Rolling Stone* in striped purple socks and silver Mary Janes. But, when I extrapolate beyond parasocial relationships and pedestals, I remember that Lauryn Noelle Hill was never placed on earth to sustain the hopes of an entire collective, was never some bloodless avatar of neo-soul. Maybe after sharing her miseducation so generously with us, we had no right to demand more. We should be so lucky. What a treasure: to be so wise that even your miseducation is a gift.

Love is a political act and always will be. I'm not saying Black love or being loved as a Black woman is some despairing vortex of lonely nights and bruised mornings. There *is* sweetness, there *is* trust, and there *is* connection. Besides, we have enough struggle-1990s R & B songs to tell those sad love tales. If love has been hard for you, it's not just because you didn't "love yourself" enough or pray hard enough or say thank you enough. It's not because you're too dark or too big or too queer or too anything. Sometimes people just suck. And I am so glad that Lauryn Hill was brave enough to name her miseducations in love—the ways exes and countries failed to love her as she deserved.

Lauryn Hill taught me one of my favorite words about love.

130

I was a pre-teen when I watched the music video featuring Lauryn Hill rising slowly with detached grace in a white silk suit. There was the nightclub scene where she, swaddled in muscular arms, her skin reflecting blue until it almost melted into cobalt, stares off into a lonely future only she was privy to. There was a word she sang that hit me so sharply, I felt it pop into my stomach.

Whenever she said this word, she sounded like someone scratched across the tender muscle of her heart, letting the sound bleed into song. I wanted to know what she longed for so deeply that her voice octaved into this fifth dimension. But, I also didn't want to know, because maybe I already knew—beyond syllables, beyond letters. But, I listened to the song repetitively until I was sure I heard right, ran my finger across the CD liner notes of "Ex-Factor" until I found the word.

I will always be thankful that Lauryn Hill taught me the meaning of *reciprocity*. This is the distance between what we give and what we receive. Some may call those of us who acknowledge this distance, and who refuse to shrink our desires, "bitter"—but I will always call us brave.

HONEYKNIFE PRAXIS

- **Drip:** Write a short thank you note to someone and send it. Too many of us don't receive our flowers while we can still admire them. Reverse that tradition.
- **Drizzle:** Keep a gratitude journal for a month, recording what you're grateful for and why. Writing down why we're grateful for something helps us key into what experiences we'd like to repeat and how.
- **Pour:** Donate 5–10 percent of your income to a cause or person you care deeply about. Sharing from our excess is an awesome way to pay our gratitude forward.

10

The Oprah Ache

"It was a *Beloved* moment, if you know what I mean: the daughter who comes back from the dead."
—Oprah Winfrey[35]

One day, in the sunny apex of almost noon, my nanny showed me a Polaroid of my mother. I and my nanny were sitting in her peach living room on her velvet couch. Family photos and oil portraits of scary white angel children decorated her walls. I am tempted to set this scene in sepia because her living room contained multiple shades of rust. My nanny was a white woman who many called Mrs. Bowers and we called Nan. She looked very British—silver blunt hair, colonial pink skin, stare like a dagger dipped in milk. I lived with her and her own small family, I remember a daughter and a special needs son, alongside my uncle Femi and my cousin Dayo, in a small southern England town called Havant.

My Havant memories are sparse. I remember overeating Flintstones Vitamins and a handful of visits from my family in London. I fed horses sugar cubes at the nearby stables and visited the beach, hating the feeling of seaweed licking the soles of my feet. My nan was the one who read Mother Goose nursery rhymes to me and picked out the splinters in my soft palms that I got from playing outside. We were a delightfully odd found-family

---

35 "Oprah's Family Secret," Oprah.com, January 24, 2011 (http://www.oprah.com/oprahshow/oprahs-family-secret/all).

reminiscent of a progressive 1980s sitcom.

My parents moved to California when I was seven months old: my dad for work and school, my mother, like many women of that era, to follow her husband and start a family. Immigrating as an African was already enough of a complication without bringing a baby along. I wouldn't see my parents again until I was nearly four years old, but this sort of setup is kind of normal in immigrant families. Sisters grow up half in and half out of the family structure. Brothers go without seeing each other for decades. You discover a random cousin in your thirties. And so, I stayed behind in England with Nan. In the few photos I still have from this era, she is often cut out of the frame, but her arms hold me close in the shielding stance of mama bear.

That day when Nan showed me the photo of my mom, I leaned in close enough to smell my nan's soft soap. The photo was a tiny Polaroid passport spread of a pretty woman with cavernous brown-black eyes, a soft round face, and crimson lipstick.

"This is your mother," Nan said. "Yomi."

I ran my hand over the glazed surface. "Yomi," I repeated.

"No, you don't call her that. You call her Mum," she said.

Baby Oprah has eyes like my mother. Pregnant eyes. In photos of the girl who would become the first Black woman billionaire, Oprah Gail Winfrey's eyes are dark almonds heavy with wisdom and maybe just heaviness itself.

We know Ms. Oprah as the titan businesswoman and philanthropist, the always available ear to both Hollywood glitterati and, more recently, British royalty. Since the 1980s, Oprah Winfrey has connected with viewers not with the usual salacious talk show BS but by sharing real stories about child abuse, sexual trauma, and domestic depression. In a particular episode, white women bonded with Oprah over her weight struggles, cheering her on as she rolled a red wagon full of an artificial configuration of the fat she lost in a diet across her stage. They sobbed on her shoulder and confessed their gutter-bound secrets on her couch.

Oprah Winfrey's mother, Vernita Lee, was single and a teenager when she brought her child into the world in Kosiuko, Mississippi, in 1954.[36] Oprah spent her early years with her maternal grandmother on a small farm, a woman whom Oprah credits with instilling an early discipline. Oprah eventually reunited with her mother in Milwaukee when she was six years old. At the time, her mother was working long hours as a maid and boarding with a very light-skinned woman who did not want a brown-skinned girl sleeping inside her house. Baby Oprah was sent out to the porch that night instead.[37]

Since the inception of her career, Oprah has been accused of playing mammy to the nation, a neutral maternal figure who ignored complex social issues in favor of a more individualized self-empowerment path with a side of goop. Many who criticized her seemed to forget that thriving in an economic world built for the comfort of whiteness was and is a David-and-Goliath balancing act.[38] People also seem to forget that the mammy is an invention that had little to do with the real needs and desires of Black women.

Right now, probably in a duplex not too far away from you, there's a Black woman taking care of someone else's kids. She's a daycare worker, a grandmother, a fulltime babysitter, a nanny teaching her boss's daughter Dominican-inflected Spanish. She is being paid almost nothing, minimum wage, or her generous Silicon Valley employers match her 401(k). She's returning home to a host of people who rely on her labor—her own children, nieces/nephews, husbands both useless and doting, aging parents.

We know the mammy figure as the desexualized ubermother, always

---

36 "Oprah's mother, Vernita Lee, on motherhood, her Milwaukee history," video, *ABC Wisconsin*. Originally aired May 23, 2004 and April 20, 2007.

37 Lisa Capretto, "The Night a Young Oprah Was Sent to Sleep Outside on a Porch," *Huffington Post*, October 13, 2015.

38 Tammy Johnson, "It's Personal: Race and Oprah," *Colorlines*, December 15, 2001.

ready and eager to serve. Even in the fake world of Hollywood, where we have recreated Godzilla for the zillionth time and somewhat realistic CGI abdominals, the mammy trope has had a slow death. In 1939, Hattie McDaniel won the Academy Award for Best Supporting Actress for playing the subtly named character "Mammy" in *Gone with the Wind*, becoming the first Black entertainer to ever win an Oscar. In its over 90-year old history, the Oscars has repeatedly crowned Black women for playing mammy adjacent roles (see Whoopi Goldberg as mystical maternal guide to Patrick Swayze in 1990's *Ghost* and Octavia Spencer in 2011's *The Help*).

While these actresses gifted their roles with a nuanced humanity, we deserve to witness Black women beyond matronly advice giver. The persistence of the mammy myth and the way this myth bleeds between our artificial and very real worlds means huge segments of our population will never have to grow up. Keeping the mammy myth alive fuels strategic incompetence on the collective level.

But, in the United Kingdom from the 1960s through the 1990s, there was a *totally* different reality going on. Thousands of African diasporic children, mainly Nigerian, were being fostered by white families and white mothers in particular. The arrangement took the cringe name of "farming" and was often an arrangement the professionally mobile and college-educated Nigerian class could afford, but even less economically stable parents planned childcare this way. The caregivers, like my nan, were often working-class white women in outside London towns. During the popular days of farming, *Nursery World*, a "weekly magazine for the care and upbringing of children" occasionally published articles about the intricacies of caring for Black children. Articles like "Curly, why do you need more vitamin D?" gave white parents advice on proper sunshine intake, combing "frizzy" hair, and the near heavenly benefits of Vaseline. Month after month, in the cramped back pages of these magazines, alongside classifieds for prams, dozens of parents posted weirdly specific childcare ads.

URGENTLY WANTED, NICE FOSTER MOTHER in our home near Liverpool for Nigerian boy (5 years) and girl (2 years). Both parents post-graduate students.
FOSTER FAMILY wanted for two West Indian children, age 5 and 17 months, two boys.
FOSTER MOTHER wanted for a 5-month-old Biafran baby girl, Christian family preferable.

Some stayed with their foster families indefinitely, others returned *mostly* well-adjusted back to biological families. Then there were the stories of children descending into sharp mental distress. Turns out raising Black children in rural England during Margaret Thatcher's golden age wasn't a recipe for positive emotional development. There are a lot of sad stories. In 2018, actor Adewale Akinnuoye-Agbaje released a feature film about his own harrowing experiences growing up alongside a skinhead gang in right-wing England. Nigerian-British comedian Gina Yashere spent several months with a nanny. Author Precious Williams[39] wrote an entire memoir about her own complicated experience being fostered by a white family.

I talked to Precious Williams over terrible Wi-Fi in a noisy Costas Coffee once. It was almost as if Williams and I were on a girlfriend date. We made small talk about Erykah Badu. She was pretty and round eyed with her locs piled high in an elegant top knot, a red lipstick to match her turtleneck. I was in a turtleneck too, green, but she was in London and I was in Havant. We talked via our respective screens, hers a laptop, mine a stubborn iPhone.

Williams is the author of *Colorblind*, a 2010 memoir that details her experiences as a farmed daughter. She is a busy writer and activist; we were unable to meet in person during my brief week in England because she was

---

39 Precious Williams, "If I was precious, why did she send me away?" *The Telegraph*, July 12, 2004.

attending a women's rights march and was traveling to Sierra Leone a few days later. I read Williams's work in 2016 and instantly felt recognized by the candor in which she described the acute longing for her birth mother, her honest portrayal of maternal rejection. Our experiences are similar in that we are both Nigerian daughters (she Igbo, me Yoruba) who bonded well with our stand-in white mothers. Her foster home was located just one train station away from Havant in nearby Petersville.

Williams was eventually adopted by her foster parents after a chaotic hearing; her story is rife with sexual abuse and complicated feelings about her nanny (her nan gave her the nickname of "Nin," unfortunately short for pickaninny). Farming is not a practice that Nigerians are wild to talk about—if they know about it at all. There have been several times I have explained this foster care system to Nigerian friends who had no idea.

Farming occurred alongside Enoch Powell's 1968 Rivers of Blood speech and a large uptick in neo-Nazi organizations during the 1970s and early 1980s. Margaret Thatcher was prime minister from 1979 to 1990. I asked Williams why Nigerians thought leaving their kids with white people in towns that overwhelmingly voted "leave" during Brexit was a good idea.

Williams laughed gently before answering. "In Nigeria, there is this extended family to take care of kids. I think at this time, Nigerians kind of looked to England almost in a parent-child way. They wanted access to the English way of life and most planned to eventually come back for their children," she says.

Innocence is a huge feature of farming. My aunts describe their shock and delight when they first heard my uncles speak in the crisp British accent. "Briti-co!" they shouted anytime my uncles said a word. Williams's own mother wanted her to develop a Queen's English accent. Even though she considered herself to be much higher in class than William's nanny, she was enamored with the clear, polite way the nanny spoke. It's an as-similation story most immigrants know: trying to make a way where there is none, stuck between a rock called nationalism and your own dignity. While Williams does believe that some of these parents knew they were sending their kids into harm's way, she also stresses that the numbers of willfully negligent parents was a small minority. "But, I still think a lot of them feel guilty now," she adds.

Not too long after my nan introduced me to my mother via Polaroid, I left Havant for good. I didn't know this would be the last time seeing my nanny, and she didn't know either. My mother, terrified that my nanny would try to gain custody if she hinted that my trip was a one-way ticket to Los Angeles, told my nanny that I was visiting family in London.

I don't remember the first time I saw my mother upon arrival. My mother speaks about this day often: how relieved she was to see me in my backwards baseball cap and overalls; how my father picked me up and spun me around and then remarked to my mother that I needed to lose weight (thankfully this was out of my earshot).

We were strangers to each other. I wondered when this strict Nigerian lady was going to return me back to England and my "real mother," and she wondered whether this odd child who conversed with roses and couldn't keep a McDonald's burger down to save her life was actually hers.

My mother is a Gemini on the cusp of Cancer who taught herself to drive late nights when she first came to the United States when my father was too work tired and irritable to play instructor. We have the same apple cheeks and share a tendency to cry at airports. She put herself through nursing school and has traveled to every country I have ever resided in, usually with Tupperwares of jollof rice in tow. She is delicate, yet strong, and decidedly hilarious. Once, when I was a teenager, I asked my mother if women were second class citizens in Nigeria, she said no of course not, they were *fifth* class.

When I first arrived in America, my mother would ask me the same two questions.

"How much do you love me?" my mother would ask.

"This much," I'd say and then I'd hold out my hands to sapling width.

My mother would then ask her next question, "How much do you love your nanny?"

"Like this!" I would say without a trace of social awareness and zero chill, throwing out my arms wide enough to carry the sun, moon, and the stars.

My mother laughs when she tells this story. I am both embarrassed by my social obliviousness and wish she never asked me the question in the first place. There was no good answer. At the time, my nanny was the only mother-figure I knew. Even if our bond was not biological, she was the one who read me nursery rhymes and tried and failed to do my hair, settling on a neatly trimmed Octavia Butler afro and never attempted much else.

My mom and I had an origin story that was the perfect recipe for a mother wound—too little support and so much need for the both of us. Every morning before preschool, my mother would remind me to greet my teachers. I was so scared of my mother, so desirous to please her, that I would say hello to the thin air when I exited the van. My mother would look at me with the look I often elicited in her—a mix of annoyance and disbelief that she could have birthed a daughter so daft.

At this point of my life, I have gone through enough therapy to know that my mother was mothering through her own girlhood pain. She was busy with my younger sister and brother who were born in my absence. Being that they were still toddlers, they demanded the lion's share of her attention. She was moving through a complicated period with my dad as they gained their footing in a country where strangers at Kmart asked them if they were related to Shaka Zulu. There was a tenderness, a patient witnessing I sorely needed at the time that my mother could barely afford to give to herself.

According to spiritual teacher Bethany Webster, the mother wound is ". . . the pain rooted in our relationship with our mothers that is passed down from generation to generation in patriarchal cultures and has a profound effect on our lives." Webster takes care to define the mother wound across a variety of levels to include the personal, the cultural, the spiritual, and the planetary.

The mother wound tends to be cavernous for Black women who are working across multiple layers and intersections. First off, we don't play when it comes to our mothers. To criticize your mother, to disparage the womb that formed your life, is tantamount to the greatest of all disrespects, especially considering that some mothers provide the ultimate sacrifice and leave this earth to bring us into this world.[40]

In the most industrialized country on earth, Black mothers with higher college education face the same birthing outcomes as white women who didn't graduate from high school.[41] And yet, Black women are also the racial group most likely to have children. Yoruba people place motherhood as the Mount Kilimanjaro of female achievement. My aunties were addressed as "Mother of _____," as in Iya Kemi or Iya Ibeji (meaning mother of twins), as a first name. Infertility-as-curse is a popular Nollywood film trope, and a child-free woman is seen as a deficient woman who should be prayed for, pitied even. She is a woman who will forever be only a daughter.

My mother wound is just scalped tissue, a tender buzz of neon pink with a side of *The Breakfast Club*. My mother wound is foster care and being the "bad" girl who told the truth to Child Protective Services.

My mother wound is learning that my nanny may have taken on being a foster mom to have a host of "playmates" for her special needs son. Another one of my uncles, my uncle Sunny, was once fostered by my nanny for a bit alongside his younger brother, my uncle Femi, the uncle I spent most of life in Havant with. My nanny, seeing that they were speaking Yoruba to each other and thinking this would halt their learning of English, sent

---

40 Birthing outcomes and realities for Black mothers in the United States are improving in some sectors because of the heart centered work of Black birthing justice leaders, doulas, lactation specialists, and midwives. They are changing the world at the very onset, dedicated to the holistic health of Black mother and child. (J.C. Oparah and A. D. Bonaparte, *Birthing Justice: Black Women, Pregnancy, and Childbirth*, New York: Routledge, 2016.)

41 Nina Martin, ProPublica, and Renee Montagne, "Nothing Protects Black Women from Dying in Pregnancy and Childbirth," *NPR News*, 7 December 2017.

my uncle away. He cycled through a series of white families with multiple instances of what can only be described as racialized abuse.

My mother wound is sexist church politics and the murmur of misogyny that keeps women like my mother overworked, undervalued, and distant from their own dreams.

Oprah went back and forth between her mother and father for years. She had two other siblings on her mother's side, Jeffrey and Patricia. While living with her mother, she was sexually abused by male relatives, ran away from home, engaged in "wild" behavior, and even gave birth to a stillborn child, a son, at the age of fourteen. It was at fourteen that Oprah went to live with her father, Vernon Winfrey, and her stepmother, Zelma, in Nashville.[42] She writes, "My mother didn't have the time. She worked every day as a maid. . . . I was smart and my mother, because she didn't have the time for me, I think, tried to stifle it." In the early 1990s, Oprah's sister Patricia sold the story of her famous sister's secret baby to the tabloids for $19,000, further deepening a rift between the sisters.[43]

Your mother may be the first "it's complicated" relationship you know. When you pause at the site of mother-daughter hurt, you are untangling the legacy of your inheritance and what it means to be a woman—the good, the bad, and the ugly. In our most primitive being, our earliest microscopic bodies, we share a cellular environment with our mothers before our mothers are even born. While our mothers are hanging out in our grandmother's amniotic fluid, three entire generations share a home simultaneously. The mother wound is basically like those vintage store Matryoshka dolls.

Female-sexed people can trace their maternal ancestry through their mother's line, a line that is lost if she should only have sons. Male people can trace their ancestry on both sides because they have both an X and Y

---

42 Jill Nelson, "The Man Who Saved Oprah Winfrey," *The Washington Post*, December 14, 1986.

43 Ginger Adams Otis, "Oprah's Painful Years" *The New York Post*, May 27, 2007. https://nypost.com/2007/05/27/oprahs-painful-years/.

chromosome pattern. While mothers pass their mitochondrial DNA to their sons, these sons (mostly) cannot pass mitochondrial DNA onward. Once a new maternal ancestor is introduced into a genetic tree, the mother line is diverted to this ancestor's mother line and her mother and her mother. All human beings have an ancestor nicknamed "Mitochondrial Eve." This ancient woman, who originated in what is now East Africa, is not exactly the first woman on earth, but she is currently known as humanity's common matrilineal ancestor.

If you're terrified to go into your mother wound, please do not take this as weakness on your part. If you want to unpack the intricacies of your mother wound, you are not selfish or overly sensitive. This wound can be a raw place, one that has not been broached for most of history. Instinctively, I knew that my mom did the best she could with what she had. But the hurts of our earlier relationship still hurt.

I think most daughters with a mother wound know our mothers were humans doing the best they could, but our knowledge about the contextual ways abuse occurs does not disappear the pain. It can be hard to address the truth of our relationships when so much about the mother-daughter bond is shrouded in hyperbolic Hallmark cards and breathless exhalations of sacrifice.

Unfortunately, under-mothered daughters do not make cute life choices. Our naked need is a silent siren that attracts people and situations who sense our god-shaped hole. We may confuse adoration or admiration with love and spend lifetimes sprinting towards anything that barely smells like the love we so deeply want and need.

Are you my mother? Are you my mother?[44] we ask our Gucci bag, our collagen count, those sugar cookies, our waist-to-hip ratio, some random dude on Tinder, our graduate degree, our everything.

Will you love me forever and ever and tell me that I am enough?

---

44 Also the title of a great mother-daughter themed graphic novel memoir by writer and artist Alison Bechdel, *Are You My Mother?: A Comic Drama* (New York: Houghton Mifflin, 2012).

We run to spaces and people that reject, abandon, and neglect us on all levels, repeating the same painful pattern of our initial mother wound.

We feel that unless we are perfect and shining brighter than every star in the sky, we do not deserve to exhale. We punish our bodies and undermine our talents with a host of addictive or unhealthy habits. When we are in our under-mothered state, we are a naked, crying child searching for the nearest pacifier but never gaining true relief.

It is scary as hell to admit, but the one person who symbolizes unconditional love can never meet the full extent of this need—they are only human themselves. It's a trick of patriarchy to believe otherwise. And we, Black daughters with strained or complicated relationships with our mothers, face a double bind. We not only have to deal with our earthly mothers, we also have boyfriends, supervisors, strangers, husbands, partners, and even friends who wish us to perform an empowerment spell and nurture them into the next phase of their lives.

Are you my mother? they ask.

The answer of course is no—or maybe even hell no, depending on the petitioner. For many years in my healing journey, I ran circles around anything to do with the mother wound. I feared being an ungrateful, Westernized daughter who had no real complaint, especially since women from my mother's generation faced even more grievous hurts from their mothers. Instead of sitting with this part of my past for real, I made half-hearted pitches about forgiveness and complained about how stuck I felt. On Mother's Day 2015, two friends who didn't know each other sent me the same article about the mother wound.[45] By then, I had been entertaining a low-key obsession with the Goddess, studying the power of the feminine divine. The otherworldly Goddess is often where many daughters venture first when they are meeting their mother wound (flower crowns are a lot more enjoyable than unpacking complex trauma), and there was a

---

45 Bethany Webster, "Mother Wound Healing: Why It's Crucial for Women," https://www.bethanywebster.com/about-the-mother-wound/. Retrieved January 29, 2021.

lot of daughter pain that terrified me.[46]

But I had a good therapist and host of ambitious ancestor guides who desired that I heal beyond the superficial. I read feminists like Audre Lorde, Maya Angelou, and bell hooks, all women with complicated mother-daughter relationships of their own, who opened my eyes about the unfairness of what is placed on mothers and female caregivers and how to rise into a new story. I sat with brave Black women willing to face the realness of what they experienced with their mothers, and this gave me the bravery to plumb the depths myself. I accepted my limitations and that of my mother. I grew up.

Some years ago, I wrote my mother a letter about our relationship. I probably cribbed the format from some self-help book I was reading during the time. My mind was a haze of static, and I almost didn't hand it to her. I waited by the paneled doors of my living room, wondering if I should even bother. I didn't want to hurt her and maybe the letter was extra. But, right before I beat it back to my bedroom, she asked me what I had in mind—as if she were reading my heartbeat. And so, I handed her the white envelope and, in the most awkward way possible, fumbled through a summary of what was inside.

I tried to stem the staccato pulse of my heart as she read the letter. I looked at her hands, the soft brown and the half-moon scar I know came from a Snapple bottle mishap. I swallowed. Moments later, a tear rolled down her cheek, "I'm sorry," she said, "I'm sorry." And something in me that had been holding its breath for three decades finally found new air.

Daughtering is an active verb. I will not tell you that addressing your mother wound will be an easy fix, that within weeks you and your mother will be giggling over pineapple mimosas and posing for Mommy-and-Me

---

46 "... daughtering is not passive. In fact, it is quite subversive, watchful, and clandestine for the sake of survival. . . . [T]he black daughter is quite knowledgeable—she is the knower, yet always mistaken for the known. She is power." Venus E. Evans-Winters, *Black Feminism in Qualitative Inquiry: A Mosaic for Writing Our Daughter's Body* (Chicago: Illinois University Press, 2019).

selfies with nary a bad vibe between you. Sometimes in our hasty desire to move on, we bypass the harder emotions and the maturation they require and wonder why we keep hitting the same stumbling blocks in life.

The way forward with your own mother wound, whether your wound is deep or a series of papercuts, is to fully address the gaps, the impasse between what you needed and what you received as a daughter. This is slow work, tender work, divine work. If we descend from patterns of neglect, we eat with reverence and guard our sleep. If we had moms who yelled at us, we sing kind things to ourselves. If our mothers did not accept our bodies or sexuality, we practice loving ourselves just as we are. If we were expected to be perfect before we were loved, we accept our "good enough" and praise our efforts. If we had mothers who had no boundaries, we practice the fine art of saying no.

Know that you never have to do this work alone. There are professionals out there who can help. Friends who will cheer you on. Surrogate mothers who may appear in the form of peers or angels who love on you as you are. If you are a mother, you have even more incentive to meet your mother wound and create a new legacy for those who came from you. Every mother deserves to be mothered.

My mother wound urges me to be softer with myself. When I get caught up in some inner critic carousel, which still happens, I slow down enough to know that this is my past hurt daughter begging for witness and gentleness. I breathe into her truth, and then I ask her what she wants. In her own time, she always tells me exactly what I need. My mother wound beckons me to accept my inheritance, my nanny, my foster care stays, the ways that these experiences still mark me for better and for worse. I will be forever be thankful to my nanny who cared for me when I needed a mother. I will be forever amazed at the woman my mother, Yomi Shokoya Eko, has become.

Your healing is how your mother wound finally becomes mother scar.

Meet your mother wound as she is and know that complete forgiveness is not necessary. If no or low-contact is what works for your peace, then this may also be your path. When we take time to heal our mother wound, we are soothing the wounds of the first Eve, this first African mother whose children now cover the planet. We remember the bitter alchemy that produced the first wound, and we practice doing differently until our practice becomes a life. The daughter in me cheers for the daughter in you. Even though I have made much progress, this healing is a lifetime practice.

In 2011, Oprah Winfrey found out she had another sister. Her mother had given the child up soon after birthing her during a time when Oprah was living with her father in Nashville. In a bizarre set of circumstances that sounds almost like a Lifetime special, this estranged sister eventually found her famous birth family. She was initially rebuffed by her biological mother but managed to connect with other family members. Her name was even the same as the sister Oprah actually had known, the sister who had sold Oprah's secret baby story so many years before: Patricia. (That other Pat had passed on in 2003.)

During Thanksgiving Day in 2010, Oprah and her partner, Stedman Graham, drove to Milwaukee to meet Patricia Lofton. Oprah recalls meeting her estranged sister. "It was so uncanny to us and to everybody in this family how much this Patricia looked like, moved like, talked like Pat. It was a *Beloved* moment, if you know what I mean: the daughter who comes back from the dead."[47]

The day I knew my relationship to my mother had fundamentally shifted was a simple California spring afternoon with little cloud cover and almost no humidity. There was no grand finale or convulsing sobs. My sister was taking pictures of my dad, mom, and me on the front lawn of our house for our upcoming birthdays. We were all dressed in matching ankara cloth that housed a pattern best described as a cross between technicolor leopard and LSD trip. At one point, my sister suggested that my mom and I hold hands and gaze into each other's eyes. And I remember my

---

47 "Oprah's Family Secret," Oprah.com, January 24, 2011 (http://www.oprah.com/oprahshow/oprahs-family-secret/all).

mother's eyes, the altar of dancing light at their center, the way that I could see the beautiful girlchild she once was. And I loved her—I loved her fully.

HONEYKNIFE PRAXIS

- **Drip:** Find a picture of your younger girl self. Gaze into her eyes and wish her peace, power, and pleasure.
- **Drizzle:** Write your mother a truth letter, then decide whether you want to give it to her or if writing it is enough in and of itself.
- **Pour:** Attend to your mother wound in an intimate container. Work with a therapist or healer who knows what they're talking about when it comes to intergenerational healing and complex childhood trauma.

Interlude 3

Interlude 3:
From Suffering to Pleasure

There was once a feud on earth against the Village of Women.[48] The Village of Women was pissed. Legend had it that they were on their periods, too, so their power was at cosmic levels.

No one could defeat the Village of Women. Understandably, the orisa were vexed. Several of them came down from the Realm of Ancestors to get the Village of Women to behave and cease being so rebellious. The women were causing chaos, and people wondered if the gods were weaker than the women.

The gods first sent the almighty warrior Ṣàngó, who tried to win over the Village of Women with brute strength. He was quickly defeated. They sent Ogun, who fashioned powerful weapons of bronze and iron in the attempt to win over the Village of Women. He returned like Ṣàngó, defeated and long-faced.

The gods sighed. They might as well try sending the goddesses.

And so, first they sent Ọya, who was often called "the woman who would grow a beard in the event of war." But like the men before, Ọya returned utterly defeated by the Village of Women. Yemọja, mother of fish herself, gathered her seafoam skirts and went down. She raged at the Village of Women with slapping ocean waves and caustic seas, but she was still no match for the Village of Women. She, too, returned defeated.

---

48 Story recounted as a combination of the stories told within F. Fatunmbi, *Oshun: Ifa and the Spirit of the River* (New York: Original Publications, 1993), and D. Badejo, *Òsun Seegesi: The Elegant Deity of Wealth, Power, and Femininity* (Trenton, NJ: Africa World Press, 1996).

All the while, Òsun was painting her nails a delightful shade of fuchsia. The gods had almost forgotten about her. (Do these people ever learn?) She blew on her nails, smiled, and volunteered to go. She would go to the Village of Women. And she would not return defeated.

And so Òsun blew one last soft breeze upon her nails and stood, ready to face the Village of Women. Leaving the Realm of Ancestors for Earth, she balanced a calabash of water on her head and began to dance and sing one of her favorite R-rated songs.

Some of the women laughed, while others tilted their heads in curiosity. Some others appeared angry, thinking Òsun was being an asshole. Òsun did not mind their grab bag of reactions. Looking at the women standing before her, she knew that they were all her and she was them. Òsun recognized herself in their resentment, their bitterness, their disillusionment, their fear, and their hot rage. She was not afraid of their feelings, nor did she judge them.

Òsun continued to dance. Finally, one brave woman whose foot had been tapping alongside Òsun's beat could not help herself. She tied up her skirt and began to dance too. Sometimes she followed Òsun's rhythm; other times she was content to create her own. One by one, the Village of Women followed Òsun, sometimes dancing in unison, sometimes dancing alone. Smiles began to form on their faces. They did their best not to be fearful of this new feeling, this feeling called pleasure.

During the war, they had forgotten how much they loved to dance. They followed Òsun—who is love, healing, cooling waters, and seduction— because they trusted that wherever she was, there was life itself. And so, Òsun led the Village of Women back home to themselves. (In my happy feminist version of this story, Òsun dances *with* the Village of Women. She does not create yet another formation, does not subdue the righteous anger of these powerful women with a twerk fest and some trickery. In this tale, Òsun's dance is a defiance that leads the Village of Women to uncharted territory.)

She did not defeat them. Even weapons and raging oceans could not do that. She did not attempt to dominate them. Even winds and patient intellectual conversations could not do that. She did not meet the Village of Women with more war.

She simply demonstrated her joy and asked them to join her with their dance.

Where there is suffering, there is a path towards pleasure. Pleasure is: satisfaction, joy, sensual freedom, fun, contentment, the ability to be jealous of your own life. You were made for more than suffering; pleasure is your birthright.

May your suffering lead you to your pleasure.

11

The Vagina Dialogue

I met my pussy freshman year of military school. I was nineteen years old, an anxious and reluctant first-year plebe at the US Merchant Marine Academy. I spent most of my days battling exhaustion, marching in khaki-colored formation, and scrolling through "Are You Depressed?" quizzes at lunch. Like many African-derived females, I initially tried to sidestep my emotional wounds through spirituality, namely church.

During my years at the Academy, the Christian Fellowship Club was a complicated oasis from my military school blues, the congregants a pleasant combination of Gentile kindness and Fox News values. They threw me my first surprise birthday party, nurtured me during sad Long Island winters, and introduced me to the beautiful chocolate-chip pumpkin goodness of harvest loaf.

In my off time, I read "alternative" Christian titles like *Blue Like Jazz* and took the G train to attend Revolution Church, pastored by Jay Bakker, son of Tammy and Jim, a punk-rock queer-positive house of worship in Williamsburg. My idea of Jesus was less masochistic martyr and more warm-hearted hippie who liked a good Pinot Noir, women, and being kind to poor people. I didn't fit in completely with the more conservative leanings of my school church group, but unfortunately there wasn't a "Spiritual But Not Always Religious and Deeply Wanting to Know Her Purpose" Fellowship Club at the time.

For reasons I can only describe as a wink from the goddess, our girls Bible study decided to read Eve Ensler's *The Vagina Monologues* during my freshman year. We were not some renegade band of feminists inspired by radical nuns. Our Bible study leader was a born-again virgin, and I'm sure many of my classmates later enthusiastically voted for Trump in 2016. Nevertheless, we formed a group and persisted.

Ever the dutiful nerd, I followed Ensler's vulva gazing invitation. She said every woman, every human being with a vulva, needed to gaze upon her vagina if she wanted to be whole. Tall order, but I was in. And so, one night soon after our girls Bible study, I went into my dorm room, breathed a sigh of relief that my roommate was probably on some treadmill, promptly locked the door, grabbed a compact mirror, and pulled down my athletic shorts, compact mirror balanced precariously.

I wanted to see technicolor clouds and hear a remix of Maya Angelou's "Phenomenal Woman" when I looked at my vulva, but unfortunately, nineteen-year-old Hannah did not see Mickalene Thomas's "Origin of the Universe."[49] The Khia[50] anthem "My Neck, My Back" did not wail in her heart. Alone, shorts scrunched around my ankles, all I felt was a slightly disgusted shrug.

Having a vulva is strange business. There's the word *pussy*, for starters. Even after decades of repetition, it's still not one of my favorite words, but she's growing on me. Besides, *coochie*, *down there*, *cat*, *cunt* aren't much better. A rather extensive list of slightly or overtly misogynistic songs that I will still bump up to high volume in my car use the word *pussy* to describe weak behavior, pussy is a noun and adjective usually paired with active verbs like *dig*, *tear*, *beat*. In this chapter I slide between some of these names, allowing myself to linger in their linguistic and social complexity.

---

49 Mickalene Thomas' "Origin of the Universe" is a painting and a play on Gustave Courbet's "L'origine du monde" (1866). The portrait depicts a close up glittery view of a Black vulva and inner thighs. The figure is dark and swaddled in pale gold fabric. "Origin of the Universe" is also a 2012 art book and the name of Thomas's art show. You should google the painting (but maybe not at work).

50 "My Neck, My Back (Lick It)" is a 2002 hip hop ode to the pleasures of cunnilingus, analingus, and female sexual assertiveness. It may also be the undercover anthem of the nascent Black feminist.

In my Nigerian-American hyphenated household, hygiene was the beginning and end of all below-the-belt related conversations. I discovered my anatomy from the pink and magenta drawings of dusty health books. Growing up, I received two main messages about my vulva: don't get pregnant and do not be the girl who inspires pescatarian jokes.

Hearing Ensler express that my vulva was something more than the recipient of phallic objects and Pap smears was life-changing. I felt called to start an exploration of my own. Many moon cycles following my nineteen-year-old vulvic explorations, I graduated from the Academy, determined to love my pussy with the gravity I felt within those pages of *The Vagina Monologues*.

Over a dizzying decade spin, I all but memorized the pussy-manifesto *Cunt*. I took dance classes with motivational strippers who taught me the fine art of pussy popping. I had my vulva cast in clay and lifted weights with Ben Wa balls—I was no Tatyana Kozhevnikova, a Russian gymnast who is known as possessing the World's Strongest Vagina and could lift 31 pounds with her vaginal muscles alone, but I was on my way. I read books like *Woman, Pussy: A Reclamation*, and the perfectly named *What's Going On Down There?* I owned a rose quartz jade egg *and* a Diva's Cup. I even checked off a vulvic bucket list item and performed in *The Vagina Monologues* ("The Little Coochie Snoocher Who Could" was my piece). And while I became quite *cliterate*, there was still an intimacy I was actively avoiding.

Monologues, after all, are one-sided conversations, often theatrical, vocal demonstrations tailored for performance sometimes at the cost of personal connection. Many of us hold considerable trauma in our vulvas reverberating across generations. My first real memory of my vulva was when I was walking home in sixth grade and a red Jeep full of skater boys drove by. One of them yelled out that his friend wanted to *pop my cherry*. Being that I was twelve and relatively sheltered from sexual debut slang, I half wondered if his words were related to an aggressive sharing of candy. But there was something about the tone of his words, so hot and slapping sharp, that said otherwise. There was also the time when a man I did not know grabbed under my skirt in a Cleveland club, and countless misgendering experiences where I was presumed not to have a vulva at all. We are worlds away from our reality being a decently pleasant space for vulva. Vulvas have endured unwanted sex, harassment, existential disgust, miscarriages, yeast infections, fibroids, and endometriosis. It's enough to make anyone clam up.

And so, while I know on some level that vulvas are powerful (there is always the Olympian feature of birth should I forget), what consistently overshadowed this power was a pervasive culture of vulva sociopathy. Almost every woman I know has a story about being touched or harassed against her will. Over time, this culture of abuse has become so pedestrian that some women actively participate in their own debasement and encourage other women to accept the same.

Towards the tail end of my personal pussy reclamation tour, I visited a physical therapist. I was having the kind of bladder issues that primarily affect new mothers and sneezing nonagenarians. Being that I was neither with child or in my crone era, I was a little worried about my vulva. The physical therapist was a woman with office cubicle hair and a gallon of perk (we'll call her Zelda just to be fun), well used to the awkwardness of asking strangers if she could stick a speculum inside their vaginal canal. I scooted my bottom to the edge of the seat and tried to focus on the laminated anatomy posters on the wall. During part of the initial exam, Zelda straightforwardly placed her latex-gloved fingers inside my vagina and instructed me to do my best impression of a Kegel.

You can say I was made for this moment: knees splayed open, vagina muscles ready to be tested, under the patient stare of a white woman with good bangs. Kegels are a pelvic-floor exercise named after Arnold Kegel, a gynecologist who popularized them in 1948. They have been prescribed for urinary incontinence, improving orgasm strength, and healing the after-effects of pushing a nine-month-old child out into the world.

And so, I squeezed my vagina muscles ready for the verdict that my vulva was not strong enough. Zelda nodded thoughtfully, no doubt traversing her mind for the physical memory of the other vaginas that came before me. "Great strength," she said. I gloated inwardly, but a small tendril of my heart had a feeling that she would soon be adding "but not strong enough" to her conclusion. "Now, relax," Zelda said. I relaxed. "Um, no, relax," Zelda said, "like really let go." I tried again, a little embarrassed. Zelda looked at me with a conspiratorial spark in her warm brown eyes. If it were appropriate and not deeply condemned by a number of HR and patient-professional bylaws, I had the feeling she would have patted my knee. "The issue isn't your strength," she said. "The issue is that your pussy does not know how to chill."

Okay, Zelda didn't say that. She was a *professional* and used detailed vocabulary like *stress cycle* and *hypertonic pelvic floor*, but the sentiment was the same. Turns out Kegel exercises are often over-prescribed. What my vulva needed was *not* the vaginal equivalent of a pumping iron but something more along the lines of a Zoloft.

I don't know the distinct history of your vulva, obviously. I have no idea the private intimacies and generational wounds that dot your personal history. I hope and am sure that the vulvas in your lineage have also found happiness, delicious sex, and safe births amidst the generalized fuckery that is misogyny. I hope that you found people who respected your vulva as much as your soul. If you have encountered otherwise, I am sorry.

What I *do* know is that your vulva is yours.

It's not your father's, your uncle's, or your brother's.

Or your mother's, your sister's, your auntie's.

It does not belong to the Apostolics, the Baptists, the Catholics, or the Presbyterians.

Or Roe v. Wade.

It does not belong to your sorority, your first-born son, or your husband. No matter how many institutions and regimes have tried to convince you otherwise, no one owns that place between your legs but you. (If at any point a new lover asks *who's is this?* in the middle of sex and your first instinct is to reply *mine*, then you are on the right track.)

I'm sorry so many people made you forget your vulva was yours, but that is their delusion to unlearn. I'm sorry for the times your vulva has been abandoned and hurt. I'm sorry for all the horrendous things done to the vulva that came before you and lived around you.

Your vulva, my vulva, all vulvas and vaginas infintum deserve better than this.

You deserve more than immature hyperbole referencing Olympic swimming pools filled with female ejaculate.[51] You deserve more than pink pussy parades. You deserve Good Pussy Energy: champagne and bacon-wrapped dates, dancing with one breast out in a purple silk something, reciprocal love, silky intelligence, plum purple lipstick, pretty in pink, a certain *j'es ne quai* summertime sadness, fur coats, waterfalls, the second orgasm (and the sixth)—the works.

Your vulva is powerful. There would never be this array of power grabs (pun intended) if this space did not contain something worth suppressing. A vulva is nuance defined; she can stretch to usher in the shoulders of a newborn and constrict around a finger. She is the drop-off caravan of souls onto this earthly plane, a constant tension between terror and delight and still gentle as a throat.

And sometimes your vulva just needs a hug.

In all my protracted reclamation mania, I had never really paused long enough to ask my pussy what she actually wanted. Instead, I ran after

---

51 Another African vulva practice for reference is *kunyaza*, a traditional Rwanda sexual practice that encourages female ejaculation. "Kunyaza is not necessarily an emancipatory feminist practice; it can sit comfortably with male control over the woman's body. Yet, during sex, Rwandan women lie back to enjoy an experience which prioritizes their pleasure—not that of the so-called president of the house. Here lies the tension between the centrality placed on men executing the practice, and the fact that the ultimate aim is the woman's pleasure. In this push-and-pull between the genders, control slips between the two." (Alice McCool, "The Joys of Kunyaza: Women's Pleasure Comes First in Rwanda," *The New Internationalist*, 16 December 2017.) The practice is also centered in *Sacred Water*, a 2018 documentary directed by Olivier Jourdain, which follows radio host and sex educator Vestine Dusabe as she educates women and girls about the power of female orgasm and pleasure.

whatever "expert" seemed to be certain of their answers. Pausing and listening would have required initiating an intimacy I was largely scared of in my earlier years. Listening would have required more dialogue than monologue. In my frenetic hurry, I was replicating the same distance I had grown up with. Better for me to race around and never sink deep enough into the center of myself than to hear her yes or no.

But now I know that good things happen to me when I connect to my vulva. Sometimes I wonder if there isn't some pussy placebo effect going on, but even if this is true, I am okay with it. When I offer a hello to her upside triangle configuration of pubic hair and labia minora, I have better days—not perfect, but something akin to flow. When I tune into the truth of my vulva, to accepting and listening to this part of me no matter what, I feel centered, powerful, and alive.

On August 21, 2017, it is the day of the Great American Eclipse, a day strangers will gaze towards the sun-moon sky together. I'm in my final year of military service with the Coast Guard Reserves and in grad school for a degree in creative writing. By this point, I have spent nearly a decade building up my Good Pussy Energy. I knew my vulva was the seat of my intuition. I knew she carried a logic deeper than the mind. Whenever I checked in with my vulva, life was more like a kind ocean, less driven by fear. I witnessed her inherent power and the way she united me to a congregation of souls larger than Self. During the eclipse, I decided to follow my vulva for a day.

Every decision, from big to small, would be dictated by her.

I had a dinner date with friends in Fort Greene that night.

And so I asked my vulva, "Should I take the subway? Or the more expensive route and drive over the Verrazano Bridge, praying for a decent parking spot in busy Brooklyn?"

At the time, I was curbing my spendy ways. This travel would mean a $17 toll versus a $5 bus ride. It wouldn't break the bank, but it was a difference nonetheless. I expected my vulva to make the fiscally conservative choice, but she quietly told me I should drive. And so, even though my mind wanted to protest, I got in my Camry and took off. I arrived within the half hour from Staten Island, pulled into a rock star parking spot steps away from the Korean fusion joint, and was actually early. (Punctuality still is not my strongest virtue.) And for those of you who know downtown Brooklyn, easy and accessible parking for a mid-sized sedan is a small miracle.

My dinner date companions, Kelly and Diana, were writers I met at a New York workshop. Our dinner conversation was a delectable blend of the quotidian and the ethereal as always. As dinner winds down, I reached for my wallet, but Kelly offered to pay.

My friend was more than generous, but it wasn't like it was my birthday or something. I thanked her and soon after we hugged good-bye, I started digging around in my purse for my wallet to better position myself for the ride home, full of that satiated happiness that arrives from good friends and good food. Seconds later, I realized that what I thought was my red wallet was in fact my red journal. I headed back to the restaurant thinking maybe my wallet fell to the floor. I searched around the bathroom. I searched underneath the table. I returned to my car. I was full of a childlike embarrassment, the sort of sticky shame where you wonder if there isn't something developmentally amiss with your brain chemistry.

As cars whizzed by on Highway 278, I worried about fines and some vagabond stealing my identity. Then my day-long pussy promise nudged me with another question.

"Should I take the higher or lower portion of the Verrazano Bridge?"

The lower portions of the bridge would give me a better chance of explaining myself to the toll clerks directly and sweet talking my way out of my mistake.

But vulva was not having it.

She told me I should take the higher route, the one where you get that glittering panoramic view of New York City as it opens into the sea. I gulped. And then I followed. As I reached the Staten Island divide, a sign announced that the Verrazano tolls were now cashless. Sensors scanned your plates and they'd send a bill later. I had been away from the city for a while and hadn't seen the signs signaling the sensor change on the way to Brooklyn.

Once I was back on base, my wallet greeted me from the center of my bed.

If I had ignored my vulvic intuition from the beginning, I would have arrived at the bus stop with no wallet, forcing me to go back to the base to retrieve it. Being that the bus stop was a cool twenty-minute walk, I would have arrived almost an hour late to dinner. Perhaps Kelly would have still felt generous enough to comp a meal, but maybe not. I would have never experienced that gorgeous (albeit panicked) nighttime view of one of my favorite cities in the world.

I was completely taken care of—even in ways I was not totally conscious of and had no idea I would need.

Owning your vulva enough to trust her direction is magic, but not always straightforward. She is a truthteller, but her truth is far deeper than meets the eye. You may not know where your storyline is heading until after you drive over that bridge.

You start by owning your vulva—even amongst the reproductive wars, the inherited traumatic responses, and the hellscape of modern dating. If she bears scars, thank her for her honesty. When she feels good, offer gratitude for her poetic ecstasy. You own the way your vulva looks, her needs, her scent. You meet the ways your vulva's limits have been compromised and the ways you learned to trespass your own boundaries and the ways you've ingested the backwards logic of a world that believes they own you. When you own and accept your vulva as she is, as you are, you are creating a new inheritance.

I owe much to the nineteen-year-old I once was and that girls Bible study. Maybe it was all some quirky college mistake. But maybe we intuited that our holiness was not in some distant place, but located in our very bodies. *And oh, the places my vulva has gone.* She truly deserves her own picture book. The mistakes, the triumphs, the wrong-sized tampon mistakes. She continues to lead me past the understandable, yet limiting fears of my mind into a more expansive version of myself.

You have a roadmap, a compass that knows what's best for you. She has a lot to say to you. It is my hope that you will slow down enough to listen.

HONEYKNIFE PRAXIS

- **Drip:** Write a letter to your pussy and from your pussy. What does she want you to know? What do you want to say to her?
- **Drizzle:** Let your pussy plan your day.
- **Pour:** Get a Pap smear and then take yourself out for dinner.

12

Cherophobia

We were little Black girls on a pleather couch watching *The Little Mermaid*, a pack of practically cousins whose mothers traveled the same Yoruba baby-shower-party-wake circuit of Central Los Angeles. We bonded over Spice Girl lollipops, the itchiness of tights, and Sailor Moon. Like many young girls gamely exploring their subconscious via mythological creatures, I had long housed a soft spot for mermaids and their siren charm. I was obsessed with the Daryl Hannah vehicle *Splash* and would rewind the underwater scene in *Hook* just to watch the part where Robin Williams is given air to breathe by laughing fish-women.

Noses almost pressed to the shiny screen, we watched as our favorite oceanic redhead lost her voice and got her man. A dangerous message for lovesick preadolescent girls to be sure, but this was 1990s Disney, and Ariel was at least better than the 1950s glassy-eyed blonde princesses with too small feet. We were nearing the end of the movie, when Ariel says her final goodbye to King Triton, who gifts her human legs and a rainbow for her wedding gift. Who can forget Ariel's delight as she stands on her new legs in that sparkly slip dress, the crescendo, the hushed *thank you daddy*, the marital kiss.

Our reverie is broken when one of our aunties, probably taking a breather from adult talk and gossip to grab another Sprite, is stalled momentarily by our beatific faces. She decides she must interject. And so, she laughs loud enough for us to turn our heads, and then she issues her proclamation, "Life does not work like that."

None of us thought that we were going to become some version of Mami Wata.[52] We were just Black girls who had the audacity to desire with a hopefulness that bordered on lust. We had not yet had our dreams beaten out of our chests. We had not yet learned how terrifying happiness could be and how so many were threatened by our joy. Though we were being slowly conditioned to be fearful of happy events, to be on guard for when their goodness runs out or vanishes altogether, there still remained a spark of belief that we too could inherit joy.

When I met my first boyfriend after twenty-five long years of kiss-less-ness, I had to consult a tarot card reader and a therapist to not fuck it up. I knew myself. He was so kind. So cute. Sometimes, happiness is terrifying to me. Like, I'll wake up (already a plus) and eat something that is not donuts or air, something protein-rich and adult. An aura of pink goodwill surrounds me as I move about the most mundane tasks of the day: showering, waiting for the bus, checking an email. Or maybe it's during my stint in grad school and instead of standing in front of a classroom of dozing coeds, my students will be deeply engaged in the lesson at hand. My day is delightful, imbued with ease. "This cannot be," my Scrooge-like ego will cry, awaiting a piano to drop on my head or news of some impending environmental disaster—anything to break up the streak of goodness that has landed on my lap unearned.

Cherophobia is *a fear of happiness.* I know who I am when I am Sad Girl. I was undercover emo in junior high, listening to morose white guys wail about alienation. My favorite color was grey before an uncle told me that saying so out loud might scare people. I was a preschooler whose favorite cartoon characters were the Grumpy Care Bear, the Grumpy dwarf, and a clinically depressed donkey named Eeyore.

I don't want to know exactly what this says about what kind of trauma

---

52 African diasporic water spirit and mermaid figure famous throughout the Continent and beyond. Often a feminized spirit, she sometimes wanders amongst everyday humans and even appears in some stories as a man. Depending on her mood and the vibe, she has also been known to lure the unsuspecting (usually men in the form of sailors or fishermen) to their oceanic deaths.

I held as a kindergartner, but one thing I loved about the Winnie the Pooh gang was that Eeyore was never ostracized. He was honest in his own little rain cloud way. Like Eeyore, people with depressed outlooks tend to be realistic and adept at personal responsibility. I often equated happiness to being a little bit stupid. *Can't they see the misery in the world?* I'd think to myself. Sadness was evidence of an existential bravery, a willingness to plumb the downward valleys of life. Happy people were ignorant, superficial, and obviously in deep denial.

Being sad is my familiar sweater. Happy days, when life serves lemonade with extra sugar, is when I become a stranger to myself.

One late summer during grad school, I ventured to Detroit. I was there mostly to catch Grace Jones in concert. Also known as the Patron Saint of Alternative Black Girls, Grace Beverly Jones is a multi-faceted singer, model, actor, performer, and artist dedicated to the art of self-invention and adventure. Born and raised in Jamaica, she has made her way around the entire world. I have long admired her irreverence and her independent otherness, the way she so deeply belongs to the 1970s and '80s and skips over linear time simultaneously. She inspires me to be exactly who I am.

I also wanted to see one of America's great chocolate cities as Detroit became a haven for artists after everyone got priced out of Brooklyn and LA. I met with an old high school friend, had breakfast at a trendy diner downtown, went to a 420 yoga class I found on Instagram, and did what I always do in new cities: artfully wandered around town with headphones in, like a modern-day flaneuse with her very own personal soundtrack. Downtown Detroit holds a cheerful desolation, like a parking lot after the circus has departed. During one of my nighttime jaunts, a gorgeous homeless man serenaded me with an echoey rendition of "A Thousand Miles," by Vanessa Carlton.

Visiting the Museum of Art in Detroit, I immediately head over to the African American wing because if there's Black art, I wanna see it. The sizeable area was decorated with a detailed history of lynching and also had Billie Holiday's[53] gutsy whine singing "Strange Fruit" from a locked pallet box (on repeat). If there is another more apt picture of intersectional depression, please let me know.

At one point, probably with an overpriced museum lemonade in hand, I sat on a bench outside and wondered about happiness. *How do I sit with the horrible atrocities committed against Blackness without making this horror show the central story? What is my place as a recent, first-generation arrival into this race experiment called the United States? Who will give me the permission to have my own happy ending if it's not me?*

Then as now, I ask these questions selfishly. Eternal Sad Girl or not, I adore joy and I detest how much Blackness has become synonymous with struggle in the public imagination. I am tired of people of all hues acting as if Black suffering is the only thing that makes Black people *real*. I am tired of "what doesn't kill me makes me stronger" when the evidence also points to "what doesn't kill me might just give me complex PTSD."

I ask these happiness questions collectively. There's something of the sado-masochistic variety that's going on with an obsession on Black suffering—like maybe the powers that be are self-pleasuring at the thought of Black people, Black women especially, living lives of pain. Like maybe, in some cruel way, our pain sort of turns them on.

This overt focus on suffering is grossly overrepresented in the art world, especially in the league of literary artists whose bios often contain the words

---

53 "Strange Fruit" is a 1939 anti-lynching ballad made legendary by Lady Day, the woman and singer most commonly known as Billie Holiday. The song was penned from a poem by a Bronx Jewish man and has been rerecorded by the likes of Nina Simone and Jeff Buckley. Billie Holiday, who hated performing the song due to the terrible memories it resurrected (she lost her father due to the segregation policies of hospitals), nonetheless performed one of her most famous ballads memorably: total darkness save for a spotlight on her face and no encore. The song was so powerful that the Federal Bureau of Narcotics Commissioner Harry Anslinger forbade her to perform it, an order which Holiday consistently disobeyed. Her refusal was not without consequences: Anslinger set her up in a heroin drug sting, for which she was imprisoned. After departing prison, she was denied a cabaret license, negatively restricting her career. Over a decade later, Holiday was in ill health due to years of drug use. Anslinger handcuffed Holiday to her hospital bed and forbade doctors to give her further treatment. She died at the age of 44. (Eudie Pak, "The Tragic Story Behind Billie Holiday's 'Strange Fruit,'" Biography.com, April 5, 2019.)

"unhappy childhood." As a writer, I was taught that when things are going good on the page, they are going *horribly* for the reader, namely that they didn't care. Strife and conflict are where the action and importance is, but sometimes I also want to know about joy.[54]

Artists, activists, and academics are susceptible to acting as if evil alone is worthy of close study and intellectual focus. Our work is dedicated to finding argument and mistake, a Now That's What I Call Terror of the sociopolitical sort. And in our 24/7 digital news cycle, we are bombarded with updates to our imminent apocalypse: melting icebergs, sociopathic billionaires, reckless gun deaths, wily robots who want your job and your blood stream. Life's hardships and doomsday declarations are nothing new, but now we can scroll through them in high-definition without commercial break.

Happiness can be uncomfortable. It is scary to hope when we know the frailty of our existence, when we have felt the full blow of failures and witnessed the limitations of humans and our planet. Somewhere out there in the big blue and green, someone is always having the worst time of their life and someone is having the best.

Happiness can also be lonely. If we witnessed people in our most intimate relationships as tired, striving people or had our happiness belittled, we may push happiness away. In these ways, happiness feels akin to disloyalty. These beliefs are marrow deep, not always conscious. Sometimes our joy upsets the fragile ecosystem of our social groups; a happy Black woman is a threat to a system devoted to her unhappiness. Sometimes even our dearest friends and family prefer us when we're cynical and miserable. Sometimes we prefer ourselves this way. There are real, material ways that depression, anxiety, and trauma responses make happiness difficult, but this does not mean lasting happiness is impossible.

And I want happiness; I can't help it.

I want good weed, deep conversation, excellent sex, a planet that is not

54 Ayana Mathis, "Ayana Mathis: The Absence of Joy," *Lambda Literary*, December 11, 2020, lambdaliterary.org/2011/11/the-absence-of-joy/.

on fire. I refuse to overly rely on saccharine displays of excess (happily-ev-er-afters and rags-to-riches fables devoid of complexity) to get there. This variety of happiness is often hedonistic with the lifespan of a party weekend, contingent on an Unbothered Carefree Black Girl obliviousness I could not pretend to inhabit if I tried. I want a happiness that leaves ample room for bouts of depression, for grief, for emo eras, and my inner Eeyore.

Meri Nana-Ama Danquah's tender and honest memoir, *Willow Weep for Me: A Black Woman's Journey Through Depression*, charts her lifetime experience with depression against cultures that would like to pretend depressed Black women do not exist. Far from being a disorder, shame, or stigma, depression is a skillful somatic, mental, and emotional response to trauma. Depression is not just an individual failing, separate from the world. Women have consistently reported higher levels of depression than men, and a casual glance at Tinder, sexual violence statistics, and childcare does not make us guess too hard about why.

My last duty station was Sector New York in Staten Island. It was July 9, 2012, and the air was sticky with humidity. I was heading home after my first full day of work, dragging my rollaway suitcase up a hill to catch the 78A bus. A thought blazed into my mind with cutting clarity: *Once this tour is done, I am never doing this again*—"this" meaning my active duty service in the Coast Guard. On that happy day, I would be done with delaying my self-actualization. I would be done with the deeply baked-in institutional racism and sexism. I was done wondering "what if" about my writer dreams.

In 2015, after my service with Sector New York had finished up, I left Coast Guard active duty and moved back out West. I had been an officer for about six years and in military school for five before that. I knew even as a college freshmen at the US Merchant Marine Academy that I was never going to be a "lifer," putting in my twenty years for the promise of respect-ability and a generous pension. I had long held the dream of writing and spent much of my off-time wandering around the maze of Powell's Books and going to writing workshops. As a progressive Black woman, I wasn't exactly an ideal fit for the conformity of the military life. But truly and deeply, I left because of my happiness.

I was a mermaid who had other oceans she needed to explore.

I would caution those little girls watching *The Little Mermaid* against making a sainthood of sacrifice. I'd tell them to challenge the storylines that say that the sole purpose of Black womanhood is to serve as the helpmeet of humankind, ignoring your own joy. Black women have reached goddess figure levels of denial, our selflessness the stuff of legend, our forgiveness mythical. Our religions taught us that charity is our duty and that negating these acts means we are selfish and mean.

I don't know how *comfy* this martyrdom feels in real life, away from the weak compliments and plastic trophies, but kudos to those who desire to walk that path—because that isn't me. My happiness needs spaciousness. It is almost impossible to be happy when you are exhausted and serving everyone else to the detriment of your own soul.

I would tell those Little Mermaid girls to tend to their obligations, yes, and as much as they can, give when generosity lights up their soul—when they have the time, energy, and desire to give in the first place. Other than that, do your best to keep your good stuff for yourself and share from an overflow of your happiness.

Happiness is also about being a good loser, and being a good loser is holding space for grief. You may be scared to surf the crests and valleys of happiness and to fully embody the nadirs when they arrive. You may think you are doing yourself some big old self-preserving favor when you refuse to embody your happiness, when you downsize your dreams, but you are closing yourself off to life itself, not just the after-grief of joy.

Sometimes you will lose. You will lose partners, plush jobs, securities, your youth, money, pride, control. You will lose your magic touch and sometimes the esteem of those you hold dear when you dare to live differently.

Black people know the shakiness of collective happiness all too well. Radical Reconstruction was a period in American history immediately following the Civil War. The era was unprecedented for the movement of Black American people (mainly men) into positions of public power, with two Black men being elected to the US Senate. The 14th Amendment (civil and citizenship rights to all persons born in the United States, to include free women and men) passed in 1868, and the 15th Amendment (instituting that race was not a disqualifying factor for voting rights) passed in 1870; both Reconstruction-era legal changes. These changes were not met by a happy dance from the white majority. Reconstruction was also the era that saw the rise of the Ku Klux Klan (founded in 1866), an organization that did its savage best to terrorize Black families and curtail political and social progress.

I will not lie to those Little Mermaid girls and tell them everyone wants them to be happy. Nor will I position any numbness or heaviness they feel as their own personal failing. But I will say that when you dare to be happy, even in a world that so deeply wants the opposite, you are throwing a Molotov cocktail into the matrix. You are helping little Black girls who wanted happiness and mermaid realities to become real.

Write down what makes you happy in a cute little notebook, even if your happiness is a little offbeat. Start with tiny joys, small delights, microdoses of pleasure—titrate your happiness over time like you're reverse poisoning yourself. Instead of starting with some overly complicated morning routine involving twenty minutes of meditation, affirmations uttered perfectly over your impeccable ancestral altar, and fifteen minutes of yin yoga, maybe begin with five minutes where you don't look at your phone and instead sip a glass of lemon water. Sometimes happiness requires us to start small and even a little boring.

When you are happy, inhale this happiness all the way in, even when you feel like sprinting into next week. Let your happiness become matter. Know how your happiness dresses, puts on her perfume, laughs, plans her day. Happiness is not for the passive observer.

Dare yourself to let happiness in by reminding yourself often of the instances you have felt its presence in your life, noting them down if you feel called to—the small surprises, the intimate connections with people and beings you adore, the way the sun melts into the west like liquid carnelian.

When you find yourself wanting to dismiss another person's joy, ask yourself why. Entertain happiness even when it feels weird or makes you feel guilty. This guilt is not actually guilt but shame about needing and wanting more than you were taught to expect for yourself. Happiness is sometimes defiance; be willing to hold onto your joy even when you are used to discarding your happiness in the presence of those who are suffering.

I sometimes wonder what life experiences brought my auntie to that precise moment when she saw our little mermaid faces and decided to interrupt. Perhaps she wanted to warn us away from tidy resolutions and selling away your entire life and family for a taste of Prince Eric. Or maybe witnessing our shiny beaming faces and soft smiles startled something inside of her own heart, something so tender and aching that she could only bypass her own pain by introducing her raw heart to ours.

Whatever the stories you hold about happiness, refuse to allow a legacy of cherophobia to stop yourself from moving towards that which delights you when you can, how you can. Your happiness is to be savored and appreciated as the gift it is. While you still have breath, while you are still here, lean into the mighty emotion of happiness when it arrives.

What have you got to lose but everything?

HONEYKNIFE PRAXIS

- **Drip:** Do one thing that makes *you* happy—however small or mammoth—and luxuriate in your delight.
- **Drizzle:** Write a Happy List. Write down ten things that make you happy and make space during your day for your happiness.
- **Pour:** Design a life that centers your satisfaction, joy, ease, and pleasure. (Do not be surprised if you meet resistance inside or out.) Embrace support if you need it (therapist, counselor, or coach) to create this life.

13

The Sweetest Spell

The first day sugar saved my life I was the lone Black child in a Sunday School class of hyperactive blondes. (Cue After School Special Opening Chords.) I am seven. My family is trying out a new church. We will stay with this church for a couple of months since it is only ten minutes away from our house. We will leave this church because the membership is older than what my parents wanted and because, with the Orange County racial demographics being what they are, we resemble six chocolate chips drowning in a glass of milk.

I am hesitant to join these kids. I have never had a knack for finding my grounding in large social groups where I am a stranger. Plus, I had already experienced the intrusive questions about my hair, the width of my lips, the color of my gums. I was not exactly eager to pal up. Suddenly, a tray of sugar cookies enters the room.

The Sunday School teachers set the plate on a table. I had never had a sugar cookie before this, but they smell like sweet heaven, so I reach out and take a bite. The cookies are soft, buttery magnificence. A swell of delight erupts inside my belly and floods my chest until my head is a tingling confetti bomb. I now know that sugar consumption increases serotonin, a neurotransmitter that often enhances happy feelings. As a child, all I felt was the rocket blast of a sugar high, a high that provided a joyful comfort I could control.

After that Sunday, I searched for sugar cookies *everywhere*. (I used to feel so betrayed when I bit into what I thought was a sugar cookie only to taste the unmistakable cinnamon of a snickerdoodle.) But no matter how many I tried, each crumb left a bitter disappointment: no cookie has ever cast a spell quite like the ones I first tried at Sunny Hills Church of Christ.

I grew up in Disneyland adjacent suburbia, amidst reduced calorie margarine and cottage cheese diets. Restrictive eating was so normalized that not complaining about your desire to be thinner was seen as weird. The girls I hung out with, nice girls who stuck to the middle blur of the school popularity spectrum, were intent on thinness as a marker of pretty. I was a reader of high fashion magazines who wanted to look like Donyale Luna but always wanted more breadsticks at Olive Garden.

It was in middle school that I learned firsthand what *lanugo* was, the downy hair that anorexic sufferers often grow, as a way for their bodies to conserve the heat they lose from excessive fat loss. Sarah, one of the members of my junior high clique, never ate lunch and had lost close to twenty pounds over sixth-grade summer. I recognized the danger Sarah was toying with and her hyper-fixation on being skinny, but I also admired Sarah's steely resolve, her supernatural ability to resist the allure of chicken nugget day.

I was not so immune. I stuffed down my uncomfortable feelings (read: 90 percent of human emotion) with Cadbury bars, Knotts Berry Farm thumbprints cookies, extra helpings of jollof rice. My middle school had a small store, replete with candy bars, cookies, popcorn, and chips, called the Snack Shack, run by, no joke, the PE teachers. Snickers bars were three for $1 if you had the Associated Student Body discount. I was there every day that the Snack Shack was open, dutifully often at the front of the line.

Before my eight-minute walk home was through, all three chocolate bars would be making friends with my stomach and dissolving into a haze of jittery high.

I did most of my emotional eating this way: fast and hidden away from the judging eyes of friends and family. Eating always felt confusing. In under one hour, an aunty might announce to my face that I was getting quite fat, then urge me to get an extra helping of egusi soup; another would praise a slender cousin and then, when I express a desire to go carb free, send out a stern reminder that men don't appreciate a bag of bones. What was a girl with undiagnosed anxiety and chronic people pleasing habits to do?

While I ached to be slender like a Delia's catalog model and nursed unrealistic desires to have a full six-pack , I never could give up my loves—Krispy Kreme donuts, towering Dr. Peppers, and oven-baked instant cookies—for more than a week nor did I brutally over-exercise. Growing up, I wished I could have traded my more athletic body for my younger sister's willowy one. But I loved the comfort of Little Caesar's Crazy Bread. My eating was less Lifetime Movie eating disorder with the bells and whistles of exposed rib cages and clandestine visits to the bathroom after dinner; it was more a fuzzy hum that undergirded my entire life.

It's often somewhat easier for Black women and girls to hide addictive eating patterns. Less likely to exhibit our wounds in Adderall binges and anorexia, we rely on quieter self-protections. Eating was where we drowned our feelings of inner chaos. We ate to feel good and solid and alive.

While we may not land on the extreme side of eating disorders like bulimia and anorexia—instead quietly hiding a mélange of disordered eating styles—overeating and emotional eating are common issues in our communities. Larger women with eating disorders like bulimia and anorexia hide in plain sight since no one assumes "the big girl" could have a problem with eating.

Our emotional eating takes different shapes. We are the tired single mother bingeing on instant baked Tollhouse cookies and cheap red wine. We are the corporate girl wonder-hopping from one unsustainable fad diet (Atkins, paleo, intermittent fasting, lemon cayenne pepper fasts) to the next. We are the Type-A spiritual-bypassing entrepreneur, terrified of fat and mammification who counts her days in overly complicated vegan cleanses. We are the sensitive Black girls who drown our depression in ciabatta.

Because we have a host of public-facing political issues to deal with, our intimate, personal struggles are often sideswept to the Less Important Aisle, which means our relationship with food becomes shrouded in shame and mystery. Unlike for many white women, being big or fat does not translate into immediate social death. Our thickness (when accompanied by a flat belly, perky breasts, and a round butt of course) is seen as being in good shape. We are more likely to descend from generational lines that practiced fattening rituals than ones that bonded over softcore starvation diets.

When I was a midshipman at military school, my mom would freeze and express ship to me jollof rice, fried chicken, and baggies of garri, a starchy cassava that I adore. The post office dude would wryly send me a letter that another leaking box had arrived, and I would feel my Mom's care from 3,000 miles away. Food has not always been problem. It has also been deep love.

America, unfortunately, is quite the binary bitch when it comes to food and eating. One minute: high octane TV ads extol the virtues of a deluxe hamburger meal; the next: a body positive lingerie campaign strutting across our Instagram feed along with liposuction ads for 20 percent off. We place a high premium on healthiness looking one very specific way and associate "clean eating" and thinner bodies with a halo effect of purity, discipline, and elegance.

Even I knew that the nervy terror I felt when the Snack Shack was closed or when the Super Kmart ran out of Cadbury bars was a bit, well, *intense*. There were lonely after school days where I would be close to tears when I realized I was not going to be ingesting my trio of Snickers that afternoon. Unfortunately, instead of believing that I needed support, I settled on my old reliable crutch: there was something deeply wrong with me, and my sugar attachment was Exhibit A.

Intuitive eating, holistic health counseling, body-positive nutritionists, meal planning, and expensive trips to naturopaths across my teens and twenties were just some of the ways I tried to fix my emotional eating.

Turns out, there is a very lucrative industry of professionals who are more than happy to tell a woman how to eat.

I had some successes to be sure. From my year-long work with a holistic health counselor whose flyer I found at a plus-sized vintage store, I learned how deeply entwined my fears around eating were tied to my terror of taking up space. Intuitive eating taught me that assigning moral judgments to food was an extension of diet culture. Chocolate iced cupcakes never killed anyone, so I could stop calling myself "bad" for wanting them.

When we are stuck in addictive patterns around food, it's easy to think that the solution is more control. That if you could just "get it together" or stop being so overly indulgent, you'd instantly transform into one of those sensualist (probably French) women who eats rolls of brie for breakfast and guzzles Cabernets for dinner and never worries about the number on the bathroom scale. But, if your eating issues were really that easy to "solve," you probably wouldn't be going down Ozempic rabbit holes.

If you are constantly locked in self-sabotage patterns when it comes to your eating habits, you are actually engaged in a holy act of self-protection. There is something your body is distracting you from, something where focusing on your food habits is infinitely easier than facing what is truly ailing you. As much as you may think otherwise, your relationship with food and your cravings are genius level smart.

Your body *chose* the most accessible entry to quell her boredom, stuff down her anger, soothe her sadness, numb her discomfort. Your body speaks a nonverbal language whether you are the kind of woman infatuated with intermittent fasting, the one who cannot go a day without Diet Coke, or the one who ignores her growling stomach..

Your body, your cravings, and your eating habits are speaking (she may be yelling at this point). It is time to gently break open that spell that food has put you under, the ways that food (and thinking, fantasizing, strategizing, bargaining, obsessing about food) has provided temporary solace for.

Sugar[55] addiction and emotional eating is not a demon or a sin; these are external manifestations, telltale signals that consistently communicate what you *also* desire: rest, energy, safety, sweetness, and joy.

To this day, if I am having a hard day, due to stress or homesickness, garri soaked in water with a side of fried meat makes my heart do a happy dance. I love the interplay between the sugar I generously add to my garri and the oily salt of the chicken or beef. I love the thick texture of the garri that almost feels like cold Cream of Wheat. Every single time I have this light meal, so simple yet so succulent, there is a peaceful pleasure that my body dissolves into, a reminder of my mother's love. And, well, I am a daughter with a mother wound as wide as Saturn, so sometimes for a moment, unconditional love looks like sugar and fat and starch. Every moment I am eating, my pain is oceans away, never to be felt again.

So please, no more beating yourself up for hiding away those sleeves of Oreos or the way you cannot enter a restaurant without plotting out calorie limitations. What and how you eat has everything to do with how conflict was processed in your home of origin, whether you are neurodivergent or neurotypical, how close you live to a food desert, how safe you feel in the world, how you deal with stress and your body's needs.

Many of us become developmentally arrested with our food choices, stuck in repetitive loops where our food replaces the nurturing we missed and still need today.

---

55 "One obvious result of slave labor was the transformation of Western tastes. What, for instance, could be more British than a sweet cup of tea (the tea, imported from China, sweetened with slave-grown sugar)?" ("Slavery in the Americas" via slaveryandremembrance.org.) The beginnings of the Transatlantic Slave Trade are marked by a cruel sweetness. Sugar (or "White Gold" as British colonists called it) was a much-desired product that instigated and necessitated an influx of enslaved people throughout the Americas, but especially in Brazil and the Caribbean. While less labor-intensive than cotton or tobacco, sugar work was tended by field slaves and was harsh, intricate, and demanding. In 2014, Kara Walker's "A Subtlety, or the Marvelous Sugar Baby" was a short walk away from my Brooklyn apartment but I never had the opportunity to see the 35-foot tall "Mammy" sculpture constructed via a mix of resin, sugar, and Styrofoam. I did get a kick out of her follow-up film to the installation (she secretly taped attendees of the show) and what strange behavior a sugary vagina elicits from grown adults.

To break any spell, you need magic.

Your magic is not your staunch attempts at change, the cleanses, Monday declarations to be "good this week," the calorie counting, or any colossal but ultimately misplaced effort to control your appetite.

Your desires are magic—specific, honest, and powerful—and knowing what they are is all you need to break the spell. There is power in your cravings, whether your appetites tend towards Cadbury crème eggs or kettle chips. Part of the reason I crave sweets is that I live in a body that is a high processor and there was a well of depression underneath my anxiety. Sugar provides me with quick bursts of energy and a warm distraction from the unkind aspects of life I am unable to face unchaperoned.

Linger with your cravings. Listen to their wisdom. Learn their shapes. Do you crave sweet or salty? Crunchy or smooth? Cold or hot? How is food helping you avoid uncomfortable feelings? What are your obsessive thoughts about your size really pointing towards? How are these cravings telling on your deeper needs?

Food will probably always be my favorite way to reliably calm my nervous system. My love of sugar got me through the emotional hellscape that is middle school and through the social discomforts of military life. And while I am grateful that I had the sort of environment and intergenerational blessings that made it unlikely that crack cocaine was my drug of choice, I also recognize that healing addictive patterns around food can be thornier.

Under most circumstances, we do not *need* meth or vodka or gambling to live, but we do need food. Unless you have entered breatharian levels of spiritual awakening, a girl's gotta eat. Meeting our desires for what they are, every time we decorate our plates is a recurring opportunity to meet our present tense self.

One night, in my early twenties and alone in the quiet of my Portland apartment, I turned off the TV. I put my phone and my *Bitch* magazine in another room. I wanted zero distraction for the act I was about to complete. I sat down at the dinner table, facing the back of my purple couch, determined to feel the fullness of my emotions as I ate without intrusions.

My plate was piled with chow mein or white rice or sauteed broccoli or a burger. I don't recall the food, only that I was determined to eat slow and without interruption. I can still remember how tight my solar plexus became, how much my thoughts skipped ahead into rumination about the fat content of my meal.

And in the quiet of my evening dark apartment, I fully felt all the fear that danced around the edges of my eating habits. A holding of breath. Worries about becoming too big to be loved. A tight band across my upper stomach. A tenseness. It was this wavy fear that had been following me ever since those sugar cookie days—this was the discomfort I spent years suffocating and running away from.

Slowness was an accessible action that helped me to know my desires enough to accept them. Slowness helped me taste my food, digest it, and meet the reality of what I desired. Slowness breaks the spell of unconscious eating and the belief that I can escape the terror of being alive by controlling what goes into my mouth. Slowing down, I felt that teenage girl aching for the relief of Snickers bars and I thanked her for keeping me alive.

Over the long experience of writing and revising this chapter, I have eaten a ten-piece chicken nugget meal with a large Dr. Pepper and three McDonald's chocolate chip cookies. I have eaten avocado toast sprinkled with cayenne pepper and lemon juice on sourdough bread. I have had Perrier, an organic dark chocolate bar, and an acai bowl topped with peanut butter and bananas.

When I can remember, I slow down no matter what I eat. Highly restrictive diets and self-admonishment have never helped me for long. Slowing down and meeting the spell I thought food could fix is what works for me. None of us have the same exact relationship with food, so I cannot presume to know what you and your unique history needs. I do know you deserve to feel nourished and trusting of yourself. You may need extra support and other methods beyond slowness, but slowing down could help you get clear about what you truly need.

Sometimes, when I sit before a plate of food today, I remember that little girl wolfing down sugar cookies, the girl who knew that a sugar cookie was a more reliable friend than a judgmental first grader. I wish I could tell her that she would be okay, whether those Sunday School kids turned out to be friend or foe. I wish I could tell her it was okay to be weird and totally herself, that the right ones would accept her. I wish I could tell her that her cravings were nothing to be ashamed of and that she did not have to suffer alone. I wish I could give her a different spell that protected her soft heart beyond the meal in front of her. She is with me every time I eat. When I remember, I pat her hand, I wipe the crumbs off her face, and I fill her need for sweet comfort with a love infinitely more cosmic than a cookie.

HONEYKNIFE PRAXIS:

- **Drip:** Slow down and savor your food—no matter what it is. Notice the texture, temperature, flavor, spices, and pause whenever you like.
- **Drizzle:** Let your intuition guide your food choices for a day or a week. How did it feel to let go of should and shouldn'ts? What did you notice about your cravings?
- **Pour:** Work with a holistic health counselor, Overeaters Anonymous support group, or a health coach who has invested in culturally-sensitive, trauma-aware methodologies.

14

Built for Comfort [56]

"A ki I wo ago alaago sise
Never carry out your duties using someone else's watch."
—Yoruba proverb

People say "pillow princess" like it's a bad thing. Like being the partner who receives so well it feels like a giving is somehow a curse. I honestly do not understand that for the life of me. Like, I understand this idea of selfishness in the light of a union where reciprocity is completely lacking. I understand that taking and taking without giving is a terrible omen for a relationship. However, comma, there is something so tender, so alive, so present tense when we treat time like a lover and perfect our art of reception. There is something so beautiful when we move at the pace of comfort.

I had my first kiss when I was twenty-five. I am a late bloomer, a sunflower that somehow only opens at night, but this fact has not meant

---

56 A blues era euphemism, a body was either "built for comfort" or "built for speed" when it came to sexual experience. According to Dr. Emily Nagoski, a sexuality researcher, human sexuality is made up of three distinct systems: enjoyment, eagerness, and expectation. Enjoyment is based in our pleasure (or disgust), expectation is based on anticipation (or dread), eagerness relates to our desire to move towards what turns us on and to want more of it (or move away and want it to stop). See Emily Nagoski, *Come As You Are: The Surprising New Science That Will Transform Your Sex Life* (New York: Simon & Schuster, 2015). Rushing through life is akin to having a lot of mediocre or bad sex—sure you get the numbers (Achievement as Hyper Playgirl), but oftentimes at the expense of feeling good (Enjoyment as Slow Seductress). When the circles of enjoyment and achievement overlap in our personal Venn diagram, we move closer to a realization of all dimensions of our sexuality (and our lives).

that my romantic life has been empty. I have had much loneliness, yes, but when this flower blooms, does she bloom. About seven or so years after my sexual debut, I was in London on yet another graduate school research trip, this time studying the informal foster care phenomenon called farming. In my free time, I ventured out on a handful of Tinder-initiated dates. For this particular meet up, I chose a music producer who lived in some hip side of London. I arrived before noon when the air was still fresh and slightly cold. I remember that his Tinder profile had a collection of suggestive black-and-white cartoons featuring tall women staring with Elvira eyes. Later on, I learned that these cartoons were a kink language I was not versed in completely, involving goddess worship. Music Producer Guy was very nice, with British teeth and a super cute studio apartment that featured a wall decorated with indie-art vinyl. I was nervous, but his desires were fairly straightforward. I didn't have to do anything but receive. Unlike the unfortunate prevalence of humans who treat anything other than penetrative sex as a hurried chore before the "real sex" begins, this man was dedicated to making me feel good. But his focus felt very odd at first, even a bit deviant.

I was used to having to hurry my pleasure. I was used to worrying about taking too long. I was used to giving before receiving. That day, I kept trying to intervene and reciprocate, but he was intent. Finally, I surrendered my idea of what was *supposed* to happen and leaned into what was. It was in that receptive pose of shameless pillow princess that I experienced a release so powerful, so deep and full, that I wept hot tears of gratitude—which was probably a lot to process during a Tinder hookup, but hey.

Orgasm teaches me the power inherent in slowness, about becoming so deeply intimate with life that I open up safely to receive. This is the power of moving at the speed of my comfort, of leaning into the present with something like reverence.

I was not always like this, so accepting of time and my slower pace. During my ten-year-old summer, I wanted to marry a book. The book was not especially romantic or even cute; it was dry, literally and metaphorically—a used collegiate textbook bought by my mom for a quarter, now sharing a shelf with transmission fluid and old coolers in our garage.

The book was all about human development from utero to elderly, charting when to best potty-train and what age to expect a stroke. Accompanying the chapter on female puberty was a picture of this very tan and very naked woman, with a child beside her, posing with the ocean as backdrop. The little girl is wearing corduroy overalls and gazing at the camera. The juxtaposition of the two figures, the girl and the woman, seemed like a sexual maturity advertisement.

In elementary school, I compared my puberty markers against the book's adolescent checklist chart, ascertaining if I was hitting the correct milestones properly: pubic hair (early but the book did say not to be alarmed), training bra report date, and when it was that boys would finally be taller than me. According to this health book my period was tardy and the combination of my height and voice depth was evidence of a premature freak development.

Clueless, Saved by the Bell, and *Sweet Valley High* told me that my teenage years would be a generous overflow of life altering events: brace-faced kisses, bullies, extremely specific slang, The Prom. I wanted—no, I needed—to arrive to teenage-hood present and accounted for, face free of acne, ready to take my high school throne as the Orange County version of Lisa Turtle. This book from the garage was a security blanket, a roadmap of the potential potholes. I returned to it again and again, leafing through its pages, fascinated. One day, I would not be a little kid, and the promise of young adulthood was terrifying and exciting all at once.

I am first generation. My parents emigrated to California in the mid-1980s with thousands of Nigerians eager for economic success and upward mobility. I never felt like I had the luxury of moving slow. Immigrant life, especially American Dream–desiring immigrant life, is a constant hustle, where no one can afford to fall behind. I was parented by African Baby Boomers, who were rushed out of childhood on the tails of the intense demands and destabilization that decolonization ushered in across the African continent.

Alas. I was a kid lost in daydreams and a slow walker, and I have slept soundly through California earthquakes more than once. My slowness was a liability. If *speak up* was the most common corrective issued during my youth, *hurry up* was surely second. A tendency then to rush has followed me for most of my life, punctuated with the eventual collapse when rushing was no longer an option, my body throwing a stiff middle finger before slamming on the brakes.

Each December thirty-first, there I would be, scribbling my avalanche of goals, the memory of the human development book a shadow. Time was full of pressure and armed with bullet points. The only people who seemed like they were allowed to relish in a patient pace and *take all the time you need* were the rich, the white, and the protected.

In my fantasies, I am a subject at rest, moving in luscious flow with life. I nap without guilt. I wear comfy yet sexy clothes. I daydream. I allow my projects to breathe in between sessions. I am a woman with the circadian rhythm of a wealthy island dweller, smelling the roses and cooking complicated entrees. Every year, I hoped my frenetic pacing, my multi-tasking, my overcommitment would deliver me to a paradise when I could finally, finally just chill the fuck out.

Living with the effects of trauma—historical, social, the works—has made me an expert time traveler. My mind and body escape the present moment, a repetitive limbo that never rests. Wise to the vulnerability of the present moment, bodies responding to chronic trauma unconsciously attempt to correct the past that has already well, *passed*, and spend the other part of our time freezing, fighting, and fleeing to an unreal and therefore safer future, always in a rush to be anywhere but where we are.

According to normal American womanhood, I was supposed to lose my virginity in late high school, date a succession of terrible men in my twenties, venture to grad school at twenty-five, marry a decent enough dude between twenty-seven and thirty, and pop out my two-point-five children before age thirty-five.

As a result of these mandates, I had a soul sinking habit of checking the ages of women I admired—when they published that first book, birthed their children, snorted cocaine at Studio 54—against my own age. *Should I already be dating "the One"? Was it juvenile to go after my dreams past twenty-five? Was twenty-nine too late to try Schedule 1 substances?* [57]

Women are held hostage to time in ways remarkably different than men. We are said to become women at our first period and to cease usefulness after our last—as if our blood were two small punctuations marks time-stamping our sell-by date. There was an article in the *New York Times* about the discovery that female chimpanzees go through menopause, much like their human kin. This finding troubled earlier notions about the "grandmother hypothesis," which speculated that female humans live beyond their reproductive years to care for young because chimpanzee daughters often move away from their mothers. The subtext of this research, why don't women just die after their baby-making years are over, is stunning, but clearly articulates how deep, unreal, and disgusting the ageism women face is. It is truly a disheartening enterprise to age in a culture that only loves you when your ovaries are for the taking.

We deserve more than socially sanctioned self-loathing with burnout as the reward. We deserve to enjoy this wild ride of a life without hating ourselves for "taking too long." We deserve to enjoy each stage of our life

---

57 Drugs. Or more specifically: a US government classification assigned to the drugs with the most potential to ruin your life (and yet this list excludes alcohol). However, there is growing evidence that in controlled settings, certain drugs may actually hold the ability to help heal emotional, mental, and physical trauma. Nowhere is this more evident than with the class of drugs known as psychedelics, a type of drug that produces hallucinatory (trippy) effects. Often attached to a rather white-centric storyline (the Beats, Jack Kerouac, the Beatles, and all those 1960s documentaries you had to watch in high school), psychedelics have been used by Indigenous cultures for both ritualistic and personal reasons for a very long time to imbue the users with a sense of oneness, bookmark coming of age ceremonies, and piece a soul together. Ibogaine, a chemical compound derived from the Iboga shrub of West and Central Africa, has been used in initiation ceremonies for centuries. In recent years, some studies have shown that supervised psychedelic use may reduce the negative effects of racial trauma, depression, and anxiety in Black, Indigenous, and people of color (BIPOC) populations. (Williams MT, Davis AK, Xin Y, Sepeda ND, Grigas PC, Sinnott S, Haeny AM, "People of color in North America report improvements in racial trauma and mental health symptoms following psychedelic experiences," *Drugs* 28.3 (2021):215-226. Retrieved February 8, 2021 from https://www.tandfonline.com/doi/full/10.1080/09687637.2020.1854688.)

with a defiant joy—no matter how much our knees may ache. And since I highly doubt that homo sapiens will unite on a paradigm shift called She with the Fewest Eggs Wins, we are going to have to do most of this work ourselves.

We are going to learn how to be slow as fuck and actually like it.

The typical narrative story structure layout resembles the triangular spike of a male orgasm. It even includes the word *climax*, for goodness sake. Witness the foreplay of setting action (Act 1), the steady buildup of tension (Act 2), and finally, a volcanic eruption of said tension (End of Act 2). After this tension is resolved (Act 3), the story ends and the man drifts off to sleep (The End).

The female orgasm, by contrast, is grossly understudied and under-valued.[58] She is a tricky creature. Only in recent years have sexologists and medical researchers charted its dynamic movement. *Chronos*, a Greek word to which our understanding of chronological time is tied, is very real. The sun rises. The tides go out and in. The planet turns through space. We sing about being young forever, but our bodies gloat in their gravity. *Kairos*, another Greek word describing time, is related to a decidedly non-linear aspect of time, that *right place at the right time* magic. In its most precise usage, kairos refers to a special season that is charged with significance and outside normal time; its opposite is chronos, which refers to the drone of daily rhythm.

We are taught that chronos and kairos are enemies. But within narrative story telling, while the protagonist and the antagonist desire the same over-arching goal, be it love, freedom, or peace, their specific *actions* towards achieving the goal serve as the main differential. Chronos and kairos are organizers of time who both desire human actualization. With chronos there is safety, order, clearly defined benchmarks. Since many of us are

---

58 One of the best studies of the female orgasm is OMG Yes, a research-based group that was fed up with the stunted exploration of female orgasm. The online service both honors the unique experiences of pleasure while also demonstrating common methods that work for many female-bodied people. Highly recommend.

anxious as hell living on a rock hurtling in space, it makes sense that we desire stability, repetition, predictability. If we desire a *marriage* of time, a way of living that equally honors time-bound limits and divine timing, if we desire to live a different story around aging/rushing/FOMO, we must sink into a new love language with time, one that also honors the divinity of our kairos.

In the Hollywood depiction of straight sex, a man and a woman collapse into sweet release at the exact same time after a frenzied period of jack-rabbit humping. This rushed, unimaginative interpretation of sex performs a complicated balancing act of frail male egos and tight production budgets in under two minutes of screen time.

In real life, very few women experience orgasm through vaginal pene-tration alone.[59] The ones who do more than likely had some assistance in arriving there. The clitoris is responsible for a variety of orgasms—cervical, vaginal, G-spot—and yet is so often looked after last or ignored completely. About three-fourths of the clitoris is internal and contains as much erectile tissue as the average penis. These vast roots reach far inside the vagina, stretching like branches of a tree, a curving muscular network attached to the pelvic floor. It is her release we feel when we climax. Giving her time and permission to fill *and* feel is how we take our orgasms (and our sense of time) to an entirely new level, to a place where our comfort comes first.

Female orgasm is the priestess, a seductress of nonlinearity, and this knowledge will move well beyond the boundaries of the physical act of sex. When we get to know what really turns us on, we venture beyond the unrealistic scripts we've inherited. The more I accept the distinct shape of my orgasm, whether small, huge, or never arriving, the more likely I am to be intimate with *all* of my life. It's very hard to lie about what makes you feel good when it is just you facing you. This does not mean that you have

---

59 To be exact, 18.4 percent. (Debby Herbenick, Tsung-Chieh (Jane) Fu, Jennifer Arter, Steph-anie A. Sanders, and Brian Dodge, "Women's Experiences with Genital Touching, Sexual Plea-sure, and Orgasm: Results from a US Probability Sample of Women Ages 18 to 94," *Journal of Sex and Marital Therapy*, 44, 2018.)

to come every time to understand the power of your own divine timing. While the orgasm gap is very depressing and very real, making orgasm the north star causes *more* stress and fewer orgasms, a totality of lose-lose.

We have been hurried out of childhood, introduced to harsh truths earlier than our peers. We have been hurried to keep up with workplace schedules that fail to honor our menstrual cycles, our circadian rhythms, and our reproductive realities. We have been hurried to develop our countries to meet the standards of modern day *developed* nations without the same support, investment, and space such growth would require. We have been hurried by lovers who do not value our specific timelines.

Please do not allow your orgasm, your pleasure, to be yet another way you castigate yourself for failing to meet standards that never imagined you as an active participant.

Be with your life and your orgasm exactly as they arrive.

The less you obsess over your destination, the more pleasure you will enjoy. The more you study your specific relationship to pleasure, what turns you on, what turns you off, what helps you move into a place where intimacy is even *possible*, the better your experience will be. Becoming friends with your orgasm, the "little death," means honoring all the shapes in which your pleasure arrives: whether coy or mighty, prolonged or quick, localized or shaking from head to foot emanating power waves to the fifth dimension of the cosmos.

With this dedication to taking time with your pleasure, to moving at the speed of your comfort, you free your relationship to kairos and know intuitively that *every* minute you are alive is precious. Your chronos-based world will not make this experimentation simple.[60] We are a culture of next-day-

---

60 "I think that is something that is a part of human sexuality and it's a part of something that perhaps should be taught." These are words on the subject of masturbation from Dr. Joycelyn Elders spoken at the World AIDS Conference in 1994. Minnie Joycelyn Elders grew up in a sharecropping Arkansas family and became the first Black surgeon general of the United States. Sadly, she was strongly encouraged to resign under President Bill Clinton (four years before his own public scandal) for her comments encouraging sexual self-exploration. She was a highly decorated medical professional, an early proponent of drug legalization, and an outspoken advocate for

delivery and busyness as a marker of worth. The pain of hurrying is suffered on both an individual and collective level. Our chronos mania seriously impacts our body's timing and trust, deeply inhibiting our pleasure. Take your time to experiment with self and shared pleasuring, noting what inhibits and what expands your orgasm.

Let your kairos and your pleasure remind you that time is much more magnificent than anything a human being can lasso.

It may be difficult to walk when everyone is running, especially when your survival has been linked to being fast and first. Sometimes you may feel like a woman visiting from another time dimension.[61] Sometimes you will need to punctuate your world with flashes of hustle to stay afloat. I know you have obligations and inherited patterns that compel you to move faster than you'd like, trying to make up for lost time. Your comfort and your orgasm are the keys to moving to the tune of your own beat. No matter if you are partnered or not, young or old, grounded in this timeline or wish you lived in another era, allow your pleasure to teach you how to tell time.

The Greek word associated with the clitoris is a word closely related to key.[62] Your clitoris is a teacher, a wide open door leading you to your kairos.

Black reproductive equity: "If you can't control your reproduction, you can't control your life." (Claudia Dreifus, "Joycelyn Elders," *The New York Times*, January 30, 1994).

61 Black women are forever in time and out of time simultaneously. Imagine being born in West Africa and becoming Phillis Wheatley, a formerly enslaved girl who published her poetry in late 1700s. Imagine you are an unlettered, six-foot, dark-skinned woman named Sojourner Truth and it is mid nineteenth century and you are lecturing white women about their limited scope of female empowerment. Imagine being Gladys Betley, a cross-dressing Black lesbian blues singer during the Roaring Twenties. Imagine being Ann Petry and writing about Black sexism in the WWII years. Imagine it is the 1970s and you are Betty Davis singing about BDSM and gyrating on stage in platform boots and sequin booty shorts. Imagine being Toni Morrison and being the first Black woman to win the Nobel Prize for literature in the early 1990s. Imagine being Tarana Burke in the mid-aughts and writing "Me, Too" a decade before it became a mainstream movement. Trust your vision, your desires, and your kairos. You just never know what you are birthing into being just by being you.

62 Etymology of Pelvic Terms (Dartmouth Education), "Clitoris is borrowed directly from *kleitoris*, a Greek word for both a door-tender and the female organ. This is thought to relate to *kleis*, a key, by which one gains entrance through a door." 2008. Dartmouth Medical School. https://www.dartmouth.edu/~humananatomy/resources/etymology/Pelvis.htm.

(If you do not own a clitoris, then connect to what makes you feel the most alive, satisfied, happy, turned on, delighted, and fully in your comfort.) The clitoris is one of the only tissues of the body that does not age and rarely atrophies. Though clitorises grow over a lifetime, some women experience a loss in size during and after menopause. This shrinking of the clitoris is often due to inadequate blood flow to the area. Some gynecologists will recommend pleasure as just one of the interventions for a shrunken clitoris. (The most direct example of "use it or lose it" I have ever heard.)

Unlike the restraints of the typical male refractory period, female orgasms can occur in multiples—one orgasm setting the stage for a succession of others. Your life is not a three-cycle strict borderland of beginning, middle, and end. You are the eternal To Be Continued, a vast episodic ellipsis, always in and out of time simultaneously.

There is power in your slowness. There is a beauty to slowing down enough to receive well. There is a revolution in rest and your comfort despite the breakneck speed that our modern world is steeped in. Your desire reteaches you how to tell time for yourself and reset the clock. It's time to lay back and receive.

HONEYKNIFE PRAXIS

- **Drip:** Find a moment you normally rush through and go slower on purpose.
- **Drizzle:** Lay in bed and listen to a slow-song playlist.
- **Pour:** Take time to learn the specific language of your orgasm. What does it teach you about your relationship to time?

15

Honey Is the Knife

"When we think of the benefit bees bring, honey is normally top of the list. Yet it is only produced by a handful of bee species, and, even among these, it is much less valuable than the pollination they provide. Regardless of size, color, and social structure, bees pollinate a huge range of plants vital to humans, and without them many crops would no longer be viable. We have been fortunate to take advantage of 100 million years of evolution that have seen bees become one of the top pollinators on the planet. It is now our duty to protect them."
—*The Bee Book:* "*What is a bee?*"

Seven days after I was born, a touch of honey was placed on my tongue. In the Yoruba tradition, every new birth is welcomed with a naming ceremony. Friends and family assign the new bundle of stardust and possibility several names—or dozens, depending on the generosity of the guestlist and how much Guinness is flowing. My maternal grandfather happened to be visiting London from Nigeria the week I landed earthside. One could say I arrived with my name. My grandfather named me Bosede, which is a name gifted to daughters born on a Sunday, just like my maternal grandmother. In the rose-tinted Polaroids memorializing this day, I am in typical baby form: dead asleep, mid-cry, or just about to yawn with show of my milk-coated tongue. I am wearing a long white dress and a thin gold chain. My mother looks soft and proud with a tiny nose piercing.

During the naming ceremony, babies are also given several items to taste.

For blessings and protections. For love. Palm oil, pepper, sometimes dried fish. Salt for a flavorful life. Bitter kola nut to repel evil. Nowadays, honey isn't recommended for babies because botulism is a thing, but I am forever grateful that one of my first tastes upon entering this strange, beautiful world was the sweet, dark, and raw taste of honey. Sometimes, it feels like I have a village of women inside my heart, formidable, arms crossed in resistance. They wield swords and knives, urging me to stay vigilant and alert. They hold back breath and rein in my expression lest I be harmed. They are terrified of losing the battle that is my life. Daily, I ask myself: Do I possess the courage to meet this hard honey of resistance and anger, to finally touch the self beyond struggle? Beyond protesting, pushing, pulling, performing? Can the Village of Women inside of me ever loosen their Dahomey grip? Am I allowed to feel big and melt fully in a world that needs all the useful hands it can get? Do I have the sweet bravery to follow my bliss?

I sure hope so. I am finishing this essay, in the year of our Goddess 2023, in a weed café in West Hollywood as a quintet of bro cannabis leaders speak about $20,000 rent with the studied nonchalance of the very rich and very safe. I am drinking a glass of water and allowing myself to melt into blue dreams. Even sitting here, safe and smoking, I know the bad news: that until humans across this earth broker a new relationship to power outside of domination and hierarchy, you and I will always be in bondage, hemmed in by the limitations of some distant or nearby authority. The master and slave relationship is an existential kink, a psychological farce, but the consequences of these illusions and delusions of power are very real. The faces and handshakes may change. The colors and flags and welfare will change, but it is going to be a long while before the powers-that-be fully recognize their capacity for bliss and therefore my own.

When I was a midshipman at the Merchant Marine Academy, sometimes I'd wake up, middle of night, and I'd turn on my laptop and I'd sit there, hands poised like I was about to play a piano recital in the cold-blue glare of an empty Google screen. Back then, I could never figure out what prompted me to wake up with the unrelenting drive to search.

Today, I do know.

No matter the shape my movements have taken, no matter if I was in Italy or LA or Pittsburgh, no matter if I was seven or seventeen, I was searching for my bliss. Peace. Power. Pleasure. Underneath all the false promises, limited stories, inherited boxes—I was longing to connect to the honey that I had been schooled to forget. And it takes courage to follow your bliss. The etymology of the word *courage* is not *rage* as my inner Amazon would have definitely guessed but *cor*, a Latin word meaning heart. There is no neat little suture of honey that is going to solve what we have gone through and what we are going through. I am finishing this chapter during a season of death and unrest both afar and near, still living in the aftermath of a worldwide pandemic and far-right reactionary politics. Many of my close friends are nursing significant grief—if not for the wider political world and the layering poly-crisis, then for the private, closer wounds that weigh down spirits. Sometimes, I too want to write off bliss and the promise of Òsun as frivolous, naïve, and even unnecessary.

But, there is a Toni Morrison quote that really gets me thinking—and feeling about bliss. It is, "Female freedom always means sexual freedom, even when—especially when—it is seen through the prism of economic freedom." If a Black woman can reach the end of her life without losing her mind, her heart, or the magic diamond power simmering at the center of her thighs—she is free. Bliss is also another type of freedom. The freedom to be. The freedom to do. The freedom to have.

I love that the honey that slid across my baby mouth also made fast friends with bitter and salty and umami and acid. Perhaps my ancestors were preparing me, letting me know, "Hey kid, this world won't be just honey, but don't forget this sweetness because it belongs to you."

Òsun is often shown with a trail of bees in her wake; her mythology contains many stories of how she used her honey to seduce an adversary and transform difficult situations. One of the most common offerings to Òsun is a sweetening jar full of honey. You were born with taste receptors and senses primed to recognize the delightful, upward thrill of the sweet. Your soul knows this. Your heart too. You know that one Belinda Carlisle song "Heaven Is a Place on Earth"? I used to dance to this song in my living room because the opera of it filled me with such supernatural joy. I was one year into the world when this song burst onto pop charts. The song became one of my Spotify heavy hitters one summer when I was going through a time that was very un-honey. Very sad and heavy. Very please-let-this-be-the-part-in-the-romantic-comedy-right-before-everything-gets-better. In my Pittsburgh studio apartment overlooking Friendship Avenue and the East Liberty Whole Foods, I would put in my earbuds and I would dance.

They say in Heaven, love comes first.

I think that heaven place is within each of us.

That heaven place is our honey.

I think that honey—no matter what shape it takes—is a doorway to bliss. Peace. Power. Pleasure.

I think that when we are in bliss, we naturally attract others who have that place inside them too. We are a disparate troop of solitary bees[63] meeting at the gardenias and the roses and the marigolds and the African violets as we fill up our honey stomachs.

When I am in that bliss in me and you are in that bliss in you—we are one and we are free.

If you want to know how to find your way to your honey, to your bliss, and therefore your freedom, you must learn to follow your dance.

The first time I learned the power of the dance, I was twelve. Sixth graders at my middle school were only allowed one official dance a year.

---

63 "The vast majority of bee species are solitary. Despite working alone, solitary bees carry out more pollination globally than other kind of bee, and they are accomplished architects on a par with many of the social species. Despite the name, there is huge variation between solitary species in the degree to which they tolerate the company of others. Even without direct contact, living near members of the same species can lower your chances of predation. And if you can put up with your own family, efficiency is improved by sharing jobs. So are these groups less developed than the highly social species like honey bees? Simply put, no. Each environment has different challenges, and even within the same environment there are many ways to carve out a niche. Indeed, the fact that most bee species in the world are non-social is testament to their success." Fergus Chadwick, *The Bee Book*, (Strand, London, Dorling Kindersley Limited, 2016), pp. 20–21.

Decades later and I still remember this day. We were all so shy in our JNCO jeans and fake neck tattoo chokers, hugging the bleacher corners of the auditorium that still smelled like old lunch salad. No one was dancing. But then the DJ dropped "Feel So Good" by Mase, the 1997 hit that sampled Kool and the Gang's "Hollywood Swinging," and without prefrontal cortex intervention, I started to dance. I cannot claim the liquid facility of Ciara or the tight control of Janet Jackson nor the Vibranium coated knees of Megan Thee Stallion, but my small ecstatic bravery broke the ice and minutes later, we were all dancing, everyone suddenly free to dance like the pint-sized nerds that we were.

Dancing was when I felt untethered to my ever-present anxieties, free to float into worlds both real and unreal. In high school, I loved arriving home after school to a quiet and empty house where I could dance without a care for properness or order. I imagined myself as a silver-tongued seductress who wandered between nightclubs and seduced men with my swiveling hips.

Reality was much more complicated. For all of high school, I was a never-been-kissed virgin without a driver's license who spent too much of her computer time lurking in Adrien Brody fan clubs. My dad would rather have had me spend my extracurricular hours invested in amping up my basketball skills or studying for the SAT. His benediction after reluctantly dropping me off to some high school dance was often some judgy commentary on my mixed priorities. I would then spend much of Sadie Hawkins wondering if I was going to fail at life because I was too busy doing the Casper Slide.

There is a lovely choreography that takes place in the natural world, a waltz between flowers and bee. Flowers are the ultimate pick-mes of the plant world, enticing bees with lavish scents, purples, blues, pinks, heart-stopping patterns, and thick-fingered petals. Some flowers even go as far as impersonating female bees or loading their sweetness with nicotine and caffeine so the bees go full drunk in love and keep coming back. In exchange for the flower nectar and passing pleasures, bees ensure the flower's genetic survival through the delicate act of pollination.

When real life bees wish to alert their bee friends to the presence of flower nectar, they do so with a cool eight-figure-dance called the Waggle.[64] Dancing is their most valuable communication.

Once the foraging bee reaches the hive, they will regurgitate this nectar for a waiting house bee. It takes an extraordinary amount of intention and work for flower nectar's water content to be evaporated low enough to become the honey that many of us love. With its dark and wild taste, endless variations (whipped, honeydew, clover, cut comb, manuka, just to name a few) and ability to be used as everything from wound dresser to ritual appetizer, bees and honey are one of the many miracles of life. Even solitary bees, which make up over 90 percent of the 20,000 varieties in the bee kingdom—these bees that have no hive, no queen, and make no honey, these bees that alongside butterflies and wasps pollinate much of the earth—are indispensable to our great web of existence.[65] Almost a third of what we put in our mouths is because of the silent, diligent work of trillions of loner bees.

And so, one summer into my first year of grad school, when I read the words "honey is the knife" in an academic textbook, I highlighted the phrase in fat neon orange. The words were a celestial flirtation, suggested a pleasure beyond performance. I applied and was granted an international fellowship to study for six weeks in Nigeria in 2016. That same summer I attended the Òsun Osogbo Festival in Nigeria, where thousands of people converge on

---

64 "To keep a colony supplied with stores, honey bee foragers communicate the location of the best food sources to the rest of the hive. With no ability to talk or point at a map, they developed an unusual method of communication: they dance. The world outside the hive is bright, colorful, and three-dimensional, with rolling hills, rivers, and a lot of potential food sources of varying quality. Inside the hive, this has to be conveyed in the dark on the two-dimensional surface of the comb, and the dancing bee must translate the information using senses available to bees. The waggle dance enables a forager returning from a successful trip to convey to other foragers the distance, direction, and the quality of the food source." Chadwick, Fergus, *The Bee Book*, Strand, London, Dorling Kindersley Limited, 2016, p. 44.

65 Aditi Tandon, "No Honey, No Hives, but Solitary Bees Have Important Lives," *Mongabay-India*, March 8, 2021, india.mongabay.com/2021/03/no-honey-no-hives-but-solitary-bees-have-important-lives/.

the town of Osogbo to commemorate Òsun.

I interviewed high priestesses with cowries in their hair, climbed Olumo Rock with my sister, visited with grandparents I had only met twice before, and attended a conference about traditional African spirituality at Obafemi Arowolo University. I took Instagram-ready pictures at Òsun's Sacred Grove and ate a fish full of tiny black eggs. I knelt before the king of Ile-Ife, the city designated as the original home of the Yoruba people. I placed my legs into Ikogosi Warm Springs at the confluence where hot meets cold water but never combines.

This trip to Nigeria, my first time visiting a country I know and don't know, was one of the most phenomenal events of my life. I know this trip would not have occurred save for the love of Òsun and the careful orchestration of my family, my mother and my father, my sister, my auntie Taiwo, and the many family members who lent a kind word, housed me and my sister, fed us, made this grand tour of Yorubaland possible.

The river Òsun is where the crescendo of the festival takes place. A young virgin, called the Arugba chosen from a royal lineage, balances a calabash upon her head and leads the town on a procession towards the river. She must not trip or fall on her way there or it could mean hardship for Osogbo. Òsun as river can be full, bubbling over smooth stones, running dry and awaiting for rain. She is never wrong until we humans make her wrong.

While over 70 percent of our planet is covered by water, less than 3 percent is the freshwater we can drink, found in aquifers, lakes, and rivers. All around the world, rivers call for our attention and care. Even the majestic river Òsun, the one that feeds and heals millions, the one that those who assemble for the Òsun festival will pay for jugs to gather and rub the river droplets on their foreheads, has been polluted by nearby mining activities and a lack of investment.[66] If we do not respect and protect the many manifestations of Òsun—from river to vulture to honey to peacock to bee to

---

66 Eromo Egbejule and Festus, "The Gold and the Goddess," September 5, 2022. https://www.aljazeera.com/features/longform/2022/9/2/how-mining-polluted-nigerias-world-famous-river-and-upset-life.

sex to brass—we risk jeopardizing her very life and ours. Because when Òsun is angry, she does not play around.[67] Think massive droughts, unforgiving heat, and despair. Think uncontrollable flooding, undrinkable water, epidemics of depression. Think of this beautiful, precious Earth robbed of her sweetness.

I bought a contraband bottle of the Òsun River back with me to America, sneaking it within layers of wax prints and sweaters. I kept the bottle in a cool, dark cabinet where it shared shelf space with black castor oil and sulfate-free shampoo. Some of the reddish sand has collected to the bottom, and I know this bottle will need a refill soon. But, for the years I've kept this bottle, ferried this pocket of river from Pittsburgh to LA; she is a reminder to never forget that my freedom and bliss are always closer than they appear.

Almost four years after my Nigeria trip, I was lost trying to be found, the delicious goddess energy of Òsun only a memory. I moved back home about three months before the pandemic hit. My maternal grandfather passed away about four days into my arrival. Even though he was almost ninety and had lived a strong, long life, I had thought I might get to see him just one more time. About a week before lockdown took over the world, I attended a writing residency in Spain with guest artists so bigoted I almost wondered if there were hidden cameras secretly taping a new experimental art show called *That's So Racist.*

I was in between jobs, subsisting off of intermittent gigs, freelancing, and money from my parents. I was so anxious I could barely drive a freeway without having a mini panic attack—and if there is anything Southern California is generous with, it's freeways. My mind was an ever-present

---

67 "Whether fighting off predators, looking after their young, or protecting food reserves, bees have developed a range of powerful mechanisms for defending themselves against their enemies, be they rival insects, mammals, or other bees. A sting in the tail is the most famous defensive tool possessed by bees: an injection of venom that causes pain or death in the recipient. The delivery mechanism is a modified version of the egg-laying apparatus on the tip of the abdomen; hence only females can deliver a sting. Bees do not sting readily: venom takes a lot of energy to produce and is reserved for the most serious of threats. Contrary to common belief, in ordinary defensive situations a bee can use its stinger and fly away unscathed." Fergus Chadwick, *The Bee Book* (Strand, London, Dorling Kindersley Limited, 2016), p. 56.

fog of Worst Case Scenarios. The distress was worse at night. I felt like some kind of emotional werewolf dreading the moment the sun began his dip into sleep. I did not always do myself favors during this era, prone to fear-based decision making and frustration. I was not an easy person to be around—irritable, scattered, sometimes aloof. Goddess bless my family and friends who gave me grace and space during this time.

All to say, following our bliss, protecting our honey, will not always be simple. My bliss path has involved many missteps, misdirection, and dead ends—I have had to learn to find my own inner Òsun beat and follow with something close to faith even when my life is a dumpster fire. I am a first-generation unambiguously Black woman navigating worlds not exactly hospitable to first-generation unambiguously Black women: the military, academia, the writing world, the social justice sector, and basically anywhere where my peace, power, and pleasure is experienced as inherently threatening.

And still, I know my bliss, your bliss, our bliss is the way we heal forward and backwards in time. What do our personal histories of, trauma, abuse, and neglect rob us of?

Bliss.

What do collective legacies of oppression rob us of?

Bliss.

What does our earth give so freely and yet we find ways to punish her[68]?

---

68 "Bees are in decline across the world. Each year, we hear of more bee deaths caused by new diseases and greater habitat loss. As one of the earth's major pollinator groups, their loss poses a serious threat to the plants that rely on them and in turn everything that relies on those plants, including us. Although honey bee losses represent only a very small proportion of total pollinator declines, the catastrophic collapse of colonies experienced in some regions in recent years is a cause of great concern, with some beekeepers losing their entire stock of bees almost overnight in an, as yet, poorly understood phenomenon known as Colony Collapse Disorder or CCD. Numerous causes of CCD have been suggested, from pesticides to phone signals. It seems likely no single factor is responsible and that honey bee declines reflect pressures felt by all pollinators, but the effects have been more immediately noticeable in honey bees due to their close relationship to humans." Fergus Chadwick, *The Bee Book*, (Strand, London, Dorling Kindersley Limited, 2016), p. 58–59.

Bliss.

Bliss is an orgasmic energy of peace and power and pleasure when the borders between self and other merge into an ecstatic whole. Bliss is how we create new definitions of womanhood, motherhood, the feminine, our relationship to earth. Bliss is how you help those disowned parts of your soul come out of hiding. Bliss is the new social lubricant, better than Pinot Noir and Ice Cream Cake, a buffer to this ongoing chaos that our world is currently inhabited with. Bliss is ancestral reparations.

Your bliss is healing.

Your bliss is freedom.

Your bliss is a feeling that is distinctly yours.

During my "overeducated daughter returns home to California as the world implodes in COVID and a universal labor reckoning" phase, I spoke to a daughter of Òsun over Zoom. She was wearing all white with a sunflower bracelet, her digital background a gorgeous garden minimalist spread from Pinterest that I almost thought was real life. She is on a quest to lead Black women to their bliss, so of course I bought all her *Black Girl Bliss* books and tell my friends to do the same. On our call, we had a real talk about the wild things we've seen in the industries of pleasure: A woman running an orgasm cult and ripping people off for thousands of dollars. A famed writer whose Divine Feminine path is basically teaching lonely women to play doormat for a King.

I was on this call because a part of me still wondered if Òsun's honey was truly for someone like me. Still seduced by the idea of perfection, I held fast to the idea that my life had to be conflict-free and camera worthy, that I had to be endlessly gleeful to call myself a devotee of the bliss that Òsun so deeply embodies. After all, I am no hyper-feminine Cool Girl or frolic-in-the-green-hills witch. I am not an Ifa initiate or a community organizer feminist who communes with the ancestors over mushroom coffee every morning. "I used to think the same thing because I'm so cerebral," said this daughter of Òsun, "but I think Òsun comes to the ones who need her most."

There is no time quite like the present to follow the dance that lights *you* up—*your* inner Òsun, *your* "Heaven on Earth," *your* honey. There are many roads and expressions to Òsun, from Mother of the Mirror to the Artful Seducer. Òsun can be so old that you must ring a bell to reach her at the depths of the river and yet also so young that she still contains an innocent joy. One of the most known roads to Òsun is her role as the Owner of the Dance, *Òsun Kayode.*

Òsun is not asking you to abscond from your responsibilities or the knives you still need to protect you and your hive from harm. She is not judging you when your life is hard or difficult. She only asks that you never forget that your bliss matters.

What is more revolutionary than a Black woman who puts her bliss first? Who decides with gentle conviction to place herself at the center of her life? Pour into yourself as if you are honey, as if you are a river, as if you are a wake of alien bees following the goddess herself because you are. Observe who and what pours into you. If the honey transfer is not reciprocal, find new flowers. If you ever feel you are hunting for your honey off the bottom of your cup—that you are repeating cycles of overeating, overworking, overthinking, burnout, or bitterness—stop the scrape and start the pour.

Patience is key. Many of us are unlearning years and generations of over-stepping our own boundaries. There will be times when pouring into your bliss is easier than others. And while the trajectory of healing is definitely nonlinear and varies day by day, I have often found that attending to my bliss with rest, soothing, care, and finally pleasure, is both more kind and more sustainable than trying to do everything or succumbing to doing nothing.

The pleasure ethic of *Honey Is the Knife* is inspired by the conditions that create sexual positivity: chill, kind, and sexy.[69]

The first pour into creating and inspiring bliss is so often rest because it is difficult to be in your bliss when you are exhausted, burnt out, and sucked dry. Fall in love with the softness of night. Sleep. Nap. Stare into space and

---

69 "Exactly what context a woman experiences as sex positive varies both from woman to woman and also across a woman's life span, but generally it's a context that's low stress, high affection, and explicitly erotic." Emily Nagoski, *Come as You Are* (Simon & Schuster, 2015), p. 88.

do nothing. Daydream as sport. Close your eyes and let the sun kiss your eyelids. Press pause whenever you can. It's okay to rest and take your time.

Rest will often naturally open up to soothing your pains—the pains that you have finally started to feel after having rushed around and numbed out. As you can, tend to your emotional wounds, the psychological aches, the body's call for kindness and slow movement. Find the healers who aren't just selling unicorn farts and dopamine crashes. Talk helpfully to yourself as if your words are honey itself.

From soothing, move to care. Practice taking care of your basic needs: money, relationships, and time. Release unrealistic manifestation practices that have you building mansions on weak foundations. Extend the nurturing you so easily pour into everyone else to your own heart. Your care is recovery.

As you feel rested, soothed, and cared for, you will have more room to expand into the pleasure of your bliss—no forced entry required. Your bliss could be lighting that Egyptian Musk incense every time you come home from work. Your bliss could be quitting your toxic job. Your bliss could be a slow, succulent night drive along the Pacific Coast Highway with beach rain as your soundtrack. Your bliss could be wearing that high octane turquoise eyeshadow to the post office. Your bliss could be saying no to your friend's 346th venting session. Your bliss could be daily dancing to '90s alternative rock. Your bliss could be having a guilt-free summer fling during your girl's trip to Portugal.

In 2017, my bliss took the shape of being a featured reader for Naked Girls Reading, a nationwide movement that is exactly what it sounds like: unclothed women and gender expansive beings reading books in front of a live and eager audience. It was my birthday and a handful of my friends who had by then probably seen my pastie-covered breasts on the burlesque stage came for support. My plan to playfully drape myself with a pink silk robe I got from a thrift store was dashed when I realized that when I placed my robe on the kitchen counter, I had let its edges touch vegetable oil. Our theme for that night was powerful essays, and one of the essays I chose that night was Audre Lorde's "Uses of the Erotic: The Erotic as Power."

Lorde's essay is an inspiring call-to-action, a fresh point of view about allowing erotic energy to guide our actions beyond the bedroom. I can only imagine what this world would look like if we centered the bliss of women for real. The essay is a dense, gorgeously detailed exploration of the ways feminine pleasure has been narrowed into the PornHub snapshot, the performance of pleasure for the benefit of the observer alone. Most women are taught to be sexy but not how to tune into our own erotic needs. Within the bliss-centered ethic of *Honey Is the Knife*, you are called to pay close attention to what feels good for you.

When you have a choice, ask yourself: Is this true for me?

When you have a chance, ask yourself: Does this choice turn me on?

This is the "deep yes" that Lorde speaks about in her essay, that "internal sense of satisfaction." Your bliss is your Polaris, your North Star, moving you towards the energies, experiences, habits, thoughts, styles of clothing, spiritual practices, and people that feel good.

Our bliss, our special honey will not look, taste, smell, sound, or feel the same. There is honey that boasts the color of marigolds, honey the color of purple sunset, honey the color of blue M&Ms. I bet my honey tastes like yoga sweat[70] and the Atlantic Ocean, sugar cookies[71] and a bittersweet romance.[72] And when you poured my honey out, it would sound like a lion's roar,[73] a happy girl laugh,[74] and compassion.[75] My honey looks like the sparkle in the Black Madonna's eyes,[76] pink-purple majora minora,[77] and dark mirrors.[78]

---

70 See Chapter 2, "Slim Thick Dreams."

71 See Chapter 13, "The Sweetest Spell."

72 See Chapter 9, "Bitter Bees."

73 See Chapter 6, "Lion Daddy."

74 See Chapter 12, "Cherophobia."

75 See Chapter 5, "COMPASSION!®"

76 See Chapter 8, "Black Madonna of the Fretful Heart."

77 See Chapter 11, "The Vagina Dialogue."

78 See Chapter 1, "Mirror, Mirror, Down the Hall."

My honey feels like a slow pour,[79] a stretch that holds onto spoons. My honey smells like Black girl tears,[80] eggplant skin,[81] vetiver, and stardust. Raw, wild, and fair trade.[82] One hundred percent organic and sustainably sourced.[83] My honey is everything that makes me, everything that came before,[84] and a hint of a taste for what is to come. There is no honey in this universe exactly like my honey.

There is no honey quite like yours.

Bliss is your guide to your special blend of Òsunality.[85]

Your bliss is harm reduction for your soul, the ability to be with the bittersweet of your entire life.

Your bliss may shape shift, but there is always a door.

I didn't attend the Women's March in 2017. I could have. I happened to be staying in New York City the same weekend. I had the appropriate sneakers and righteous rage. Half of me wanted to attend. I was alarmed by the casual misogyny of Donald Trump and his grab 'em by the pussy asides like any millennial suffragette.

And yet, there was another half of me that held a quiet pause, a still and

---

79 See Chapter 14, "Built for Comfort."

80 See Chapter 4, "Crybaby."

81 See Chapter 3, "To All the Dark-Skinned Girls I Was Before."

82 See earlier in this chapter, "Honey Is the Knife."

83 See Chapter 7, "Articulations of an Afro-Romantic."

84 See Chapter 10, "The Oprah Ache."

85 Òsunality is a definition created by African theorist Nkiru Nzegwu that details an expansive view of the African erotic, an Ọsun-force which is, ". . . a dynamic creative energy connector between the intervening phases of the sexuality-fertility paradigm. In explicit terms, Òsun-force outlines a sequential energy flow from desire, arousal, copulation, pleasure, fulfillment, conception, birth, and growth. The flow need not result in conception and birth, but it does entail the principle of pleasure at the heart of copulation. This pleasure principle at the heart of the creative energy is metaphorically referred to as Òsun's 'honey' . . . Òsunality affirms the normality of sexual pleasure and the erotic. When absent in life, the result is suspended animation or stasis, as the Òsetúrá chapter chronicles, life effectively halts." (N. Nzegwu, "Òsunality, or African Sensuality: Going Beyond Eroticism," *Jenda*, 2010.)

insistent no. I felt guilty about this no, annoyed with this no. I was also curious. I knew that my no was not about my singular attendance at the Women's March; my absence would make zero waves. I also knew that I was a feminist—an imperfect intersectional feminist yes, but still wholly dedicated to the humane treatment and rights of women and nonbinary human beings.

Instead of marching alongside questionable pink pussy hats, I entered a room of hundreds of fist-pumping women and flapping feather boas. I was at a teaser event for a high-ticket empowerment program helping women embrace their pleasure. Old-school girl power anthems like "I'm Every Woman" and "These Boots Are Made for Walking" thundered through the considerable speakers. The weekend event was a mix of the radical notion that women deserve to feel good and the dopamine overdrive of large wellness events. There was a lot of screaming. We were instructed to address every woman in attendance as SG, shorthand for Sister Goddess.

I wondered if I had not made a terrible choice. I imagined the ghosts of Sojourner Truth and Funmilayo Ransome-Kuti looking down from feminist heaven, shaking their heads at my decision to forsake The Struggle for a pep rally in the key of "Wannabe" by the Spice Girls.

After a series of ice breakers and pledging allegiance to our pussies, the leader of the event, a bombastic high-femme author, addressed the elephant in the room. "Were some of you feeling guilty that you weren't at the march?" she asked with a naughty wink in her voice. "Do you feel bad that you're not marching alongside your sisters?" She then proceeded to strut across the stage, imitating the strident stride of protesters. I looked to the ceiling, waited for lightning to strike her down, but she stayed unburned. "*This* is the revolution," she said. *Okay,* I thought, not totally believing her.

This event was one year after my trip to the Òsun Festival in Nigeria. The concept that pleasure could be all I needed was alluring enough to take a crowded six-hour MegaBus from Pittsburgh to New York City but not enough to dampen the *What the fuck am I doing here?* thought obsession circling my head like cartoon birds. But I decided to trust that quiet whisper inside of me, that deliberate and soft voice telling me that if I wanted bliss, I was going to have to sacrifice the guilt, shame, addictive suffering, and perfectionism clouding the way forward.

That night I went to the after-hours event; our goddess leader had bought out a nightclub in Midtown for a couple of hours. We were instructed to let our goddess energy lead the night, to connect with what turned us on. I wore a jumbo hot pink tutu, and the bartender gave me a complimentary rum and coke. Outside this delightfully decorated Midtown haven, I knew the world was largely unchanged. I knew Donald Trump was president and that 53 percent of white women had voted him there. It was quite possible that some of those same women were currently ordering Long Island Ice Teas at the bar right at my elbow. I knew that my whole messy life awaited me when I emerged from this sacred container and that my bliss and the bliss of those I hold dear was not always going to feel accessible or accepted.

That night, I also knew I could loosen my tight knuckle grip on shame, suffering, and struggle. I could lean into my joy, even when it felt strange or inconsequential, even when other people didn't care or get it. I could look around at the women surrounding me: single moms from the Bronx, vintage punks with septum-nose rings, upper management with bobbed lace fronts, tenured kindergarten teachers with mid-back locs dyed brown. Here we were, a formidable village of women, united in feeling good. I imagined the storylines rearranging themselves to contain all the ways we were healing forwards and backwards in time just by centering our peace, our power, and our pleasure.

Our bliss was the honey; our bliss was the dance.

I danced with a woman, bald headed and tall, and we entered the middle of the circle to move our hips in slow appreciation to Rihanna's "Work." I of course broke away in shyness before the climax, but I was alive, reborn for not the last time into the possibilities of my bliss—of dancing, of freedom, of belonging. In that circle, I did not need to be anything more or less than who I was. In that circle, every one of us was free to locate the rhythm of what felt good to her bones.

The year that "Heaven Is a Place on Earth" was nominated for a Grammy for Best Female Pop Vocal performance, it lost to Whitney Houston's "I Wanna Dance (With Somebody Who Loves Me)." This Whitney standard is one of the songs I most love to dance to alone but also in the company of friends as we overenunciate the "Dance!" refrain at the very end. The song's co-writer Shannon Rubicam described "I Wanna Dance" as not just any dance. "It wasn't, 'I wanna go down to the disco and dance,' really. It was, 'I wanna do that dance of life with somebody.'"[86]

You may forget the taste of honey sometimes and that bliss is freely yours, but Òsun and her energy dares you to remember that you always have the right to pursue the dance of life, to remember that even with the shame, even with the suffering, even with the struggle, one of your first languages is also sweetness.

Your bliss is the medicine.

Your freedom is the revolution.

And your honey is the knife.

HONEYKNIFE PRAXIS

- **Drip:** Go to a favorite playlist and pick a song that you love moving to. Stop whenever you desire, sit down if you need to, but when you can: dance.
- **Drizzle:** Write down your perfect day with detail: think texture, sound, sight. Now, pick a day on your calendar and make this perfect day a reality. How did that day feel?
- **Pour:** Integrate pleasure into your life as a daily devotion. Find or create a community of people who believe in the power of pleasure. Pour into each other from your excess.

---

86 Richard Seal, *One Moment in Time: Whitney Houston* (Britannia Press Publishing, 1994).

The Honeyknife Syllabus

Further reading by chapter.

- Chapter 1. "Mirror, Mirror, Down the Hall": *Finding Soul on the Path of Orisa: A West African Spiritual Tradition*, by Tobe Melora Correa.
- Chapter 2. "Slim Thick Dreams": "An Inner Dialogue between Miami and Pittsburgh Perspiration," *Women Who Run with the Wolves: Myths and Stories of the Wild Woman Archetype* by Clarissa Pinkola Estés, and *The Body Is Not an Apology*, by Sonyee Rene Taylor.
- Chapter 3. "To All the Dark-Skinned Girls I Was Before": *Sulwe*, by Lupita Nyong'o, illustrated by Vashti Harrison.
- Chapter 4. "Crybaby": *Sisters of the Yam*, by bell hooks.
- Chapter 5. "COMPASSION!®": *Anyway: Paradoxical Commandments*, by Kent M. Keith.
- Chapter 6. "Lion Daddy": *The Pain We Carry: Healing from Complex PTSD for People of Color*, by Natalie Y. Gutiérrez LMFT.
- Chapter 7. "Articulations of an Afro-Romantic": *Woman, Girl, Other*, by Bernadine Evaristo.
- Chapter 8. "Black Madonna of the Fretful Heart": *Radical Acceptance: Embracing Your Life with the Heart of a Buddha*, by Tara Brach, PhD.
- Chapter 9. "Bitter Bees": *Shadows on the Path*, by Abdi Assadi.
- Chapter 10. "The Oprah Ache": *Sula*, by Toni Morrison, and *Dance of the Dissident Daughter*, by Sue Monk Kidd.
- Chapter 11. "The Vagina Dialogue": *Pussy Prayers*, by Black Girl Bliss
- Chapter 12. "Cherophobia": *Pronoia*, by Rob Brezny.
- Chapter 13. "The Sweetest Spell": *The Last Diet*, by Shahroo Izadi, and *Eating by the Light of the Moon*, by Anita Johnston.
- Chapter 14. "Built for Comfort": *Come As You Are*, by Emily Nagoski.
- Chapter 15. "Honey Is the Knife": The *Dirty Computer* visual and audio album by Janelle Monáe.

In Gratitude

No one writes a book alone, and nowhere is this more apparent than with the community of friends, family, and angelic strangers who made *Honey Is the Knife* possible. I am deeply in gratitude for all of your help, support, and love along this journey. It's been a doozy. Thanks for sticking by my side! I love you all. If you do not see your name here and you're my friend, I owe you a soda.

Thank you to my parents Yomi and Daniel Eko for your support, growth, and love. Thank you for the Sam's Club groceries, the fashion finds, the artistic patronage, visiting me across this nation, and for showing me that church is in your heart and an open-mind is wealth.

Thank you to my brothers, Jr. and Baba, for keeping it real, for the movie nights and the jerk chicken and the love and for your showing up in ways big and small. Thank you to the best sister in the entire world, Lolade, with your Omi Bodycare magic, your notes of encouragement, and your willingness to entertain my weed mind. *Yell yeah!* To my family around the world (especially Auntie Taiwo, Auntie Kehinde, Uncle Sunny, Uncle Femi, Uncle Segun, Aunty Jean, Bola, Jae R., Bukky of Blessed Memory, Gbenga, Shola, Banji, Lauren, Dupe, Nancy, Oju, Dame, Viola, Kabel, Ruth, Uncle Matt and Aney, Marty, David, Brandon, Auntie Dupe and your wonderful family) from Nigeria to England to New York City and beyond. I love you.

To Joshua who always believed and gave me the *La La Land* speech over and over.

Thank you to my dearest friends: Kenisha, Toccara, Chanel, 'Dre, Tanya, Amanda, Carlee, Mary, Mikael, Kelly, Diana, Theresa, Eleyna, CeCe, Nancy Z., Angela, Nancy L., Jon, Melissa, Tamera, Alex, Kendra, Kweli, Caitlin, Bibi, Alisha, Kelsey C., Tonya, Jojo, John, May, Carmen, Cathy, Shatirrie and Ms. Ski, Justin AKA Fatha Green, Jim, Thomas, Jess G., Yvonne, Ava, Suzannah, Lucia, Sam, Steffan, Jeremy, Heidi, Kelsey J., and Gayle. Thank you for your encouragement, for letting me sleep for free on your couch, for being such a beautiful example of the endless possibilities for love.

Thank you to the Scooby Doo Crew, Yoga Roots on Location, HAWT Squad, my burlesque mothers and sisters via Brown Girls Burlesque, the Velvet Hearts, and Egypt Black Knyle's #teamfuckitup. Thank you to my therapists! Like for real.

Thank you to the VONA community, Tin House, the Kenyon Review, Write Around Portland, my year-long Catapult crew, and the WOC Zine Collective. To my writing teachers: Ms. Blevins, Vicki, Ms. Row, Hasanthika, M. Evelina, Dr. Ross, Yona, Angie, Fiona, Peter, Bill, Mary, Maggie, Chaplain Sias, Jeanne Marie, Erin, Dr. Brickman, Dawn, Ms. Prince, and Kristen.

Thank you to my teachers at Penn State, Portland University, and all the writing groups who read my work. Thank you to the sociologists, historians, novelists, and artists who grounded over two hundred footnotes. Thank you to the Pittsburgh Foundation and the Advancing Black Arts grant for your generous support and the fact that I didn't have to sell my kidney to get this book done.

Thank you to Baba Elebuibon, Professor Ojujide Gbadeegesin, Iya Òsun, the African Nationality Scholarship, and all those who made that trip to Nigeria so rich.

Thank you to the most encouraging, patient editors around: Leah Lakins, Deesha Philyaw, Roslyn Richardson, Nicole Matthews, and Laura Matthews for your divine intervention. We did it!

Thank you to Tobi and Morgan of Poche for the loveliest of book covers that began this journey and for Luísa Dias for the cover design that ended this journey.

Thank you to my feline babies Everest (RIP baby boy) and Moriah.

Thank you to the Goddess, especially as She appears in the form of Òsun, Oya, Yemoja, the Black Madonna, Octavia Butler, Toni Morrison, Janelle Monae, Maya Angelou, Grace Jones, Sojourner Truth.

Thank you to the Clash, Santigold, Miguel, TV on the Radio, and all the artists who have inspired me with your work and your wonder.

Thank you to the magic of the cannabis sativa plant, especially Durban Poison, Mother's Milk, and Forbidden Fruit.

If I forgot you, I owe you a soda and I apologize. I love you.

And finally, thank *you* for reading this and making dreams possible.

Whenever I wanted to quit, I'd think of you, somewhere out there, truly caring about what I had to say. Thank you for supporting this work. I wish you bliss.

Love,

Hannah

Hannah Olabosibe Eko is a Nigerian-American writer, multimedia storyteller, and book doula. A graduate of the US Merchant Marine Academy, she holds a Master's Degree in Community and Economic Development from Penn State University, and an MFA in Creative Writing from the University of Pittsburgh. She is the founder of *The Lit Club,* a cannabis-inspired literary salon, creative community, and event series at the intersection of art, healing, and pleasure justice. Her writing has appeared in *Buzzfeed, Bust* magazine, *Fractured Lit, Aster(ix),* and elsewhere. She currently makes her home between Los Angeles and the universe.